Building Strong Relationships

By Jeremy Lopez

Building Strong Relationships

Published by Dr. Jeremy Lopez

Copyright © 2023

This book is licensed solely for your personal enjoyment only. This book may not be re-sold or given away to other people. If you would like to share this book with another person, please purchase an additional copy for each recipient. If you are reading this book and you did not purchase it or it was not purchased for your use only, please return to your favorite book retailer and purchase your own copy.

All rights reserved. This book is protected under the copyright laws of the United States of America. All information contained herein is the expressed intellectual property of Dr. Jeremy Lopez and Identity Network International. This book may not be copied or reprinted for commercial gain or profit. The use of short quotations or occasional page copying for personal or group study is permitted and encouraged.

ENDORSEMENTS

Jeremy does an excellent job of giving balanced instruction on how to meditate, and also explaining the benefits that come from having a regular meditation and mindfulness practice. I love how Jeremy is not afraid to learn from and quote those outside the Christian tradition. He is able to explain the ancient concepts simply from a Biblical perspective. – Kari Browning, Director, *The Beautiful Revolution*

You are put on this earth with incredible potential and a divine destiny. This powerful, practical man shows you how to tap into power you did not even know you had. – Brian Tracy – Author, *The Power of Self Confidence*

I found myself savoring the concepts of the Law of Attraction merging with the Law of Creativity until slowly the beautiful truths seeped deeper into my thirsty soul. I am called to be a Creator! My friend, Dr. Jeremy Lopez, has a way of reminding us of our eternal 'I-Am-ness' while putting the tools in our hands to unlock our endless creative potential with the Divine mind. As a musical composer, I am excited to explore, with greater understanding, the infinite realm of possibilities as I place fingers on my piano and whisper, 'Let there be!' – Dony McGuire, Grammy Award winning artist and musical composer

Jeremy dives deep into the power of consciousness and shows us that we can create a world where the champion within us can shine and how we can manifest our desires to live a life of fulfillment. A must read! – Greg S. Reid – *Forbes* and *Inc.* top rated Keynote Speaker

I have been privileged to know Jeremy Lopez for many years, as well as sharing the platform with him at a number of conferences. Through this time, I have found him as a man of integrity, commitment, wisdom, and one of the most networked people I have met. Jeremy is an entrepreneur and a leader of leaders. He has amazing insights into leadership competencies and values. He has a passion to ignite this latent potential within individuals and organizations and provide ongoing development and coaching to bring about competitive advantage and success. I would highly recommend him as a speaker, coach, mentor, and consultant. – Chris Gaborit – Learning Leader, Trainer

Dr. Jeremy Lopez's book Universal Laws: Are They Biblical? is a breath of fresh air and much needed to answer the questions that people have been asking about the correlation between Biblical and Universal Laws. I have known Jeremy Lopez for years, and as a Biblical scholar, he gives an in-depth explanation and understanding of the perfect blending and merging into the secrets and mysteries of these miraculous Laws and how Bible-based the Universal Laws truly are. As the show host for the past twelve years on The Law of Attraction Radio Network, this book answers questions that I have received from Christian and spiritual seekers around the globe about the relationship between the metaphysical and Biblical truths. After reading this book, readers will feel empowered and have strong faith that God has indeed given us these Bible-based Universal and Divine Laws to tap into so that we can live and create an abundant life. – Constance Arnold, M.A., Author, Speaker, Professional Counselor, Host of *The Think, Believe & Manifest Talk Show*

DEDICATION

Life on Planet Earth is filled with many wonderful and interesting people. May your life be filled with all the right ones.

TABLE OF CONTENTS

Preface	p.1
Introduction	p.9
Relationally	p.23
A Colorful World	p.37
The Power of Union	p.51
Who's In Your Corner?	p.65
Building Trust	p.79
A Return to Loyalty	p.91
The Seeds of Friendship	p.107
The Power of Openness	p.125
Giving Back	p.141
"People Matter"	p.157
Divine Connections	p.173
Conclusion	p.189

Preface

The more the merrier. In case you have yet to realize it, life on planet Earth is filled with many wonderful, interesting and unique people. These people, these characters, are part of what make life in this world such an adventure. From the moment you took your first breath on this planet until now, your life has been filled with wonderful, interesting characters. These characters, whether you've realized it or not, have served to contribute to your overall story. Though it may not seem like it now, you are writing a wonderful story. This unique story exists in part because of the relationships you have.

When I felt the inspiration to write this book, I must be honest, I thought to myself the very last thing the world needs is another book on the topic of relationships. Think of the word: "Relationships." When you hear the word, chances are your mind immediately conjures romantic connections. You think of that special someone. You envision your partner. Perhaps even the term "soulmate" comes to mind. What we often fail to realize, though, is that in this life there are many, many different types of relationships. There are romantic connections. There are platonic connections. There are the familial connections of family members. There are even business partnerships and acquaintances.

When I felt the inspiration to write this book, I knew deep down it would be time to share more insight into the meaning of all these powerful connections. I would dare to suggest that when you think of your life, your mind begins to think of the people in your life. The characters. The connections. The memories made. Stories being told.

It wasn't all that long ago that I wrote what would go on to become one of my bestselling books, *Attracting Your Godly Spouse*. In it, I shared powerful principles designed to help people attract the relationship of their dreams. Well, that is in the romantic sense, of course. To this day, it is still one of my bestselling books. There was even an accompanying study companion. If you now find yourself reading these words and are now in search of a romantic relationship, I urge you to read the book. In fact, you may be quite surprised to find that romantic connections are closer than you think. Yes, it is possible to have the fairy tale. The fairy tale of romance always seems better, though, when it's your own unique story. A story that you yourself are writing.

Love, romance and talk of soulmates aside, however, your life is filled with many other interesting connections as well. These connections, whether you realize it or not, are always contributing to the overall feeling of your life on planet Earth. With each connection and with every interaction you encounter, a story is being written. It is the story of you. The story of your life.

Like any good story though, it's only as interesting as its most interesting characters. There are heroes. There are saviors. There are knights in shining armor on white horses. Sometimes there are even villains. And yes, there are stories of passionate romance.

Life is very much like this. It's very much a very real story. With each day and in each passing moment with every person you encounter, you are contributing to the story of your life. It's good to have friends. In fact, relationships are very important. Relationships in all contexts, in fact. But I want to remind you here at the very beginning of this book, it isn't enough to have friends. You need the right ones. You don't simply need more relationships. You need the right relationships. And whether you realized it or not, you deserve those connections.

When I felt the inspiration to write this book you now hold in your hands, *Building Strong Relationships*, I wanted to share a message of inspiration with the world as a reminder to say relationships matter. Today, as you read these words, chances are some of the relationships in your life may seem a little confusing. Maybe the romance is faded. Maybe the sense of trust and a close friendship has ended. Maybe it feels you can no longer trust the person you once trusted. Perhaps it's a business associate that's causing you worry and anxiety. No matter the relationship you question in your life, those connections exist on purpose. They're there by divine design.

As you journey with me through the pages of this book, *Building Strong Relationships*, what I want you to understand is that all the connections in life matter. Simply put, relationships are heavenly. They exist in this three-dimensional world on purpose and for a very specific reason. You also are part of someone else's story. Even though you may not realize it now. You're a very important part of someone else's life. You also have a starring role to play as well. What you will soon see and realize is that there really are no coincidences. Nothing happens by chance or by happenstance. It's all orchestrated.

In order to build stronger relationships, it's essential that you begin to understand the power of relationships. There's a role that you're being asked to play. What you will soon realize is that every relationship in your life exists because you have attracted it. Although at first glance that may seem a very bitter pill to swallow, it's actually a very beautiful thing. You're drawn to certain people for a reason. You're attracted to certain people for a specific reason. You vibe well with certain coworkers for a specific reason. You have the friends you have for a reason.

And you will soon see though, you are a part of a story that's being written. And believe it or not, it's a very good story. In the story of your life, these relationships, these characters, are serving a purpose. Everyone has a role to play. When you begin to understand the true meaning of the power of relationship, not only will you learn to attract into your life the relationships you desire, but you'll begin to attract the right relationships. The truth is, you don't need more relationships, you just need the right ones.

Introduction

"The book was a lot better." I find myself saying that a lot. Chances are you do as well. Aside from being an avid writer, I'm also an avid reader. Personally, I love nothing more than a good story. As you've probably noticed, however, many times those stories don't always translate well to film. When reading a good story, so much is left to the imagination. We create beautiful stories within our minds.

Heroes. Villains. Enemies. Friends. Every good story has them all.

It's the same in the story of your life, if you really think about it. There are those who seem like heroes. There have probably been a few villains.

It may even seem that you've made a few enemies along the way. But most of all, I hope and pray that you've also made a few friends. Good friends, that is.

Suffice it to say, right now, even as you read these words, your life is filled with many wonderful and interesting characters. And if you were honest, there were also a few characters that you'd never want to see again. You've said a few goodbyes in previous chapters. You've made a few lasting connections. There are new connections soon to come. Through it all, you're writing the story of your life.

Interestingly, though, so is everyone else on planet Earth. Right now, even as you read these words, you are part of someone else's story. Somewhere, right now, when someone thinks of their life, you are a character in their story. Are you the hero? Are you the villain? Are you an enemy or friend? As much as it may seem a very bitter pill to swallow, chances are at times we're all the above. We have our good days, and we have our bad days. We have our moments. Sometimes we even do a few things we regret and wish we could take back.

What I mean to say is that although your life is filled with many wonderful and interesting characters, you also are a character in the story of someone else's life. You also have a role to play. It's one of the most powerful principles in all of existence. The principle of relationship. And though it can be a little confusing at times, and it may seem a little overwhelming, it's also beautiful if you think about it. We're really all connected.

For a moment, I'd like you to think of the most interesting moments of your life. Think back to the memories that you admire most. Perhaps it's a holiday. Perhaps it's an evening out with friends. Perhaps it's a moment with family. The truth is, if you really think about it, most of the moments of your life that matter most are as meaningful as they are because of the people in those moments.

Personally, I find it within my own personal life. As a prophetic counselor and success coach, I hear in the stories of other people the meanings of the relationships that surround them. When someone wants insight into a romantic connection or even a business deal or when someone is considering making an important decision, what they're truly asking about is the people around them. "Does he love me?" "Will she text back?" "Do my coworkers value me?" "Does my boss notice my efforts?" You see, life is really all about people. The moments we think of most are the moments filled with people.

When I felt the inspiration to write this book, *Building Strong Relationships*, I couldn't help but think to all the wonderful relationships in my own life. I think of my own friends. I think of my own family. I think of a few key and pivotal connections I've made in business throughout the years. And when I think back to the course of my life, what I find myself reminded of most is that everything matters because of the people around me. This is the power of relationship.

The truth is the life you now live on planet Earth is the direct result of connections you've made and the people that you've chosen to surround yourself with. It's time to take a long, hard look. In fact, it may even be time to make a few edits. In this chapter of your life, I want you to begin to ask yourself the question, are these quality relationships? Chances are, for a long, long time you've prioritized quantity over quality. The truth is, we've all been there, I think.

We live in such a celebrity driven culture, such a world filled with influencers, that we sometimes think "the more the merrier." We base our success on likes. We gauge status by the numbers of friends we have on social media. We seem to think the more followers we have, the better. But what I found within my own personal life and through years of success coaching, is that quality will always trump quantity. The adage, the more the merrier, isn't always true.

So right here in the very beginning of our journey together, I think it's very important to note that you don't need more relationships in your life, you need the right relationships. You don't need more people. You need the right people. You need people of quality. You need people of substance. And it should also be noted that you deserve those.

But here at the very beginning. I should probably also provide you a disclaimer. There may be a few uncomfortable moments ahead. There may also be a few bitter pills to swallow. Also, a few reality checks. The reason for this is because like it or not, your relationships are mirroring you in some way. It's always been this way, in fact.

And so, if you picked up this book in the hopes of learning secrets to change other people, well, chances are you going to be disappointed. In case you have yet to notice in life, you can't change anyone. Well, you can try. Maybe you've already tried a time or two? If so, how did that work out?

You and I aren't called to change other people. We're not here to control others. That's not relationship. It's manipulation. In case you have yet to realize it, it never works in our favor.

The principle of relationship will always demand of us that we take a long hard look in the mirror in order to see our own selves first. This is always the part that seems a little uncomfortable in the beginning. Or at least a little awkward. Most often, we would much rather look to other people than to our own selves. We love to avoid our responsibility.

Although it was written in 2018, even now I still receive testimonies from clients throughout the world sharing how my book, *Attracting Your Godly Spouse,* revolutionized their lives. I still receive testimonies, even now, of how marriages were transformed, romances were rekindled, and lives were made better. I often find it humorous, though. When the book was first released in 2018, honestly, it was a little shocking. Chances are most who purchased the book thought there would be techniques and secrets shared that might help to change the people around them. Surprisingly, though, the single greatest principle within the book is that you cannot change other people, you can only change yourself. This is why it's important to take the long, hard look in the mirror.

Now, in *Building Strong Relationships*, it's time to go even deeper. It's time to delve even more deeply into the truth of the principle of relationship. I know chances are you'd love for your partner or spouse to do something differently. I know right now there's a coworker at the office you would love to change. Chances are right now, even as you read these words, there are a few friendships you have that you would love nothing more than to completely overhaul. But what you're going to find is that this book isn't about them. This book is about you.

This book is about asking you the important question. How am I relating to my relationships in my life? As you'll soon see and discover, you've been given a very important role to play. Although you might be a character in the story of someone else's life, when it comes to your life you play the starring role. Your decisions and your actions matter. The choices you make in your relationships are of the utmost importance. The reason for this is because like will always attract like.

So, here's the most shocking, perhaps most uncomfortable truth of all. Believe it or not, the relationships in your life say a lot more about you than they do about the people in your life. If you really want to know someone deeper, simply look at their relationships. If you would really like insight into how someone is truly thinking, simply look at the people in their lives. Your relationships say a lot about you.

Do you desire more quality relationships in your life? Do you desire people of substance? Do you desire relationships filled with trust? If so, it's time to take a long, hard look in the mirror. It's time to better understand the true principle of relationship. Are you a person of quality? Are you a person of substance? Are you trustworthy?

As your journey with me through the pages of this book *Building Strong Relationships*, what you will soon find is that your relationships mirror your very own life. And if you want a difference in your relationships, maybe it's time for you to make a change within yourself first. Truly, we're all connected. We really are all one. And it's really a tale as old as time itself. What we give to others, we receive. And what we sow, we will also reap.

Right now, as you look at your life, whether you've ever taken the time to realize it or not, you are the greatest contributing factor to the relationships you now possess. Those connections aren't in your life by accident or coincidence. They're there because you've made choices and decisions. Also, they're there because you've attracted them. How are those relationships serving you? And how are you serving them?

Like I said at the very beginning, life is a very beautiful story being written. With each passing moment, your life is filled with interesting characters. But like any story that's being written, there can always be edits made. There can be revisions. Sometimes in the writing process, characters can be omitted completely. Right now, when you think of the relationships in your life, chances are there are few relationships that should be omitted. Maybe there are a few characters that should be completely cut out entirely.

The purpose of this book is two-fold. First, it is made to help you assess and realize the importance of the relationships in your life. Secondly, though, perhaps more importantly, this book is designed to help you see yourself even better than before. If you really want a better understanding of the people in your life, you need a better understanding of yourself first. If you want strong relationships, you're going to have to develop a strength in yourself also. So, the question really isn't why are these relationships in my life but rather, why am I attracting the people that I'm attracting? By understanding this, not only will you attract more quality relationships into your life, but you will attract more of the moments that feel good. After all, life is about feeling good.

Chapter One

Relationally

The self-help industry in the United States and throughout the world is a thriving, booming multibillion dollar business. And topping the charts of topics covered? Relationships. More than questions about career and finance, the burning question that seems to be at the top of everyone's mind is the question, "Is my relationship working?" It seems that much more than people have an interest in money or careers or bank accounts or cars or lavish homes, people mostly want to know about other people. This is the power of relationship.

Relationships exist on purpose. They're divine. They're neither accidental nor coincidental. They serve a very real purpose. Clearly, we all have a lot to learn.

It wasn't very long ago that life as we knew it changed, seemingly overnight. Everything seemed to stop as we entered the height of a global pandemic. Businesses were forced to shutter. Social distancing was enacted. Times of quarantine became the new norm. Some fared better than others.

Through it all, it seemed there was a cry to return to normal. In the darkest days of the pandemic, in fact, it seemed we would never again see normal. Or that we will be forced to embrace a new normal. I can still vividly remember walking through the downtown streets shortly before the closings and seeing a hand painted sign covering the door of my favorite coffee shop. "We will be back. We will see you again soon."

I would venture to guess that you saw many of these same signs in your city as well. They were standard. But as I walked through the empty streets that day, coffee was the last thing on my mind. Instead, I thought of people. If you think back to those days, chances are you felt the same. As the world seemed to beg for a return to normal, it wasn't that we were looking for a return to normal shopping days or a return to crowded malls as much as it was, we were looking for a return to connections with people. When we thought of returning to our favorite restaurants or coffee shops, the images in our minds were the images of people. Family. Coworkers. Friends.

Relationships matter. If anything, hopefully the pandemic taught us to reevaluate and better regard the relationships with the people in our lives. At the height of the pandemic, we weren't missing the moments of our former lives as much as we were missing the people in them. Suffice it to say, life is about people. And it's about how we choose to relate to those people.

It's interesting to think, if you really think about it, just how much of life truly revolves around people. Picture it. A day in your life. From the time you walk out the front door each morning to the time you go to sleep at night, your life is filled with people. And whether that feels good or seemingly not so good, there's really no escaping it.

Whether you're an extrovert who seems to make friends easily, or an introvert or loner who prefers to go through life alone, your life is still filled with people. You live your life based on your dealings with other people. Some more. Some less. And in this we find the perfect illustration of the power of relationship.

Have you ever heard the phrase they never seem to meet a stranger? You know the type. We all seem to know someone or have that one friend who can make a friend with anyone. They're outgoing and they're charismatic. They're the extrovert who never meets a stranger. Maybe you can relate to this?

And then there are the introverts. Those who seem to be loners. They don't seem to interact as publicly or make an outward spectacle of their interactions with people. It isn't that they don't care. In fact, most introverts care very deeply. They just simply prefer less interaction. And that's OK too. Really, at the end of the day, it's all about doing life in a way that feels good to you.

But there, again, is the power of relationship. And relatability. So, when I say that life is all about relationships, what I truly mean to say is that life is all about the way you relate to the people in your life. Sometimes we relate well. Sometimes we don't. I find that in life, we're all learning.

When I started writing my book *Finding Your Place* in the summer of 2021, I found myself consumed by the idea of relationship. More accurately, I found myself consumed with the idea of discovering just how exactly someone fits into the world around them. I was inspired by the idea. Deep down, no matter where we come from, we all seem to want to know where we fit into the world around us. It seems there's a desire within all our hearts to know exactly where it is we belong.

So, looking closer at this, it seems there's a sort of relationality that exists in life itself. This component of relationality is part of everything we do. Every conversation. Every initial meeting. Every conference call. Every cup of coffee with a friend. Day after day and moment by moment we are attempting to discover how we fit into the world around us. We're designed that way.

And so here we find the true meaning of the power of relationship. At the core of relationship is the desire to truly relate. It's instinctual. The desire to relate is innate. Truthfully, there's really no escaping it.

We find romance based on our ability to relate. We make friendships based on relatability. You even landed your career path based entirely on your own ability to relate to others around you. In fact, you passed the interview because of your ability to relate. Believe it or not, even though it may not seem like it now, even your boss relates to you. Well, in his own way, of course.

Personally, I believe this sense of relatability has so much to teach us, and there's so much we can learn from it. Having a better, truer understanding of relatability teaches us not only about our own selves, but also helps us to gauge the people around us better and more accurately. Relatability leads to a better sense of understanding overall. Not only a better understanding of people, but a greater understanding of the human experience in general.

So, now here at the very beginning, let's look more closely into the power of what it truly means to relate. I used the word "power" quite literally in fact. As you will soon see, you truly possess the power to change the dynamic of any relationship in your life. And as you'll soon see, you do this when you change yourself. We'll get to that part soon. But for now, back to the topic of relatability.

There's a very big difference between relationships and relatability. In fact, the two aren't always synonymous. Well, not really. Relationships stem from relatability, or from the lack thereof. A better way to explain this would be to say think of someone in your life that you don't really relate to very well. Although the relationship is there and the connection is established, you just simply don't relate well. Chances are there are also people that you once related to very well, that, for whatever reason, you can no longer seem to relate to. It happens.

Whether you find you're growing together or you're growing apart, regardless, you're still growing. That's really a beautiful thing if you think about it. All through life, our relationships grow and sometimes change all based on the needs we have where our desire to relate is concerned. The purpose of this book isn't to convince you to stay in marriages that no longer feel good, or to stay in friendships that seem to drain the life out of you and annoy you. Only you can make those decisions for yourself. No. Instead, the purpose of this book is to cause you to question how you relate in the world around you, to the people in your world. By understanding this more, you will begin to understand yourself. And miraculously, the more you understand yourself, the more you will begin to understand other people.

"Relationship" is defined in the Dictionary as "the way in which two or more concepts, objects, or people are connected." It's further defined as "the state of being connected." Interestingly, another definition that perhaps even more practical is "the way in which two or more people or groups regard and behave toward each other." Think about it. You and I are connected to people, and we behave in certain ways, based upon those connections.

But now let's take a deeper look into what it means to relate. The Dictionary defines the term relate as, "to make or show a connection between." Personally, I much prefer the other definition of the term "relate," though. Another definition of the term "relate" is, simply, "to identity with." So, there you have it. To finally begin to build strong relationships in your life, it's time to learn to recognize how you identify with the people around you.

You've been given a role to play in each of the connections in your life. So has the other person, but we're not talking about them just yet. We're talking about you. By understanding how you identify with the people in your life, you become more able to fully understand the other person as well as your own self. Discernment is crucial. In fact, this is the long, hard look in the mirror that I was talking about in the beginning.

So, you see, it really isn't that your spouse is being difficult, it's just that you're no longer able to relate. It isn't that your boss is really the villain that you believed. It's simply that you can't seem to identity with his or her behavior. And chances are he or she feels the same about you.

This leads us to perhaps the greatest truth of all where relationships are concerned. Are you ready for it? The truth is, in life there really are no enemies, and there truly are no villains. There is at times simply a lack of relatability. It's just an inability to relate or to identify with. It's as simple as that, really.

Understanding this will change the dynamic of every relationship in your life. No longer will you be content to blame others. No longer will you view others as being bad people. In fact, the truth is it's hard to judge someone when you recognize that in their life, they're simply looking for relatability also. We all are, in fact.

By better understanding the dynamic of relatability, you take control of the power of your life once more. You move from the place of victimhood once again to the place of power. You learn to recognize that you're the author of the story of your life. And most importantly. You realize that you have power and a very real say in all the connections you make on planet Earth. So, the truth is, you don't need more people to relate to, you just need to learn to relate in a better way. This is where building stronger relationship truly starts.

Chapter Two

A Colorful World

Life is truly a gift. A very beautiful gift, in fact. Well, at least I choose to believe that. If you've followed my work or my teachings for any amount of time, you know I believe in the goodness of life. I believe it's a gift from God, meant to be enjoyed and fully experienced. It's meant to be lived to the fullest.

It's really no secret, though, that life can feel good or bad based entirely upon the connections we make. There are some connections that feel good. There are others that feel not as good. Positivity aside, let's be honest. Some connections feel horrible. Or should I say that we sometimes feel horrible based on how we relate in the dynamic? Remember, no one truly has the power to change anyone else. At the end of the day, we can only change ourselves.

When I felt the inspiration to write this book, I wanted to share with the world a message of hope regarding relationships. Relationships can always change. Not because we can change others, but because we can change ourselves, thereby changing the overall dynamics and interactions in all our connections.

As much as life truly is a gift, though, it can be so easy to always dwell on the negative. To see the bad rather than the good. We're always given the choice. But something happens when you begin to see life from the negative perspective. Something that doesn't feel very good. When you look at life through the lens of negativity, suddenly you begin to view other people in a negative way also. Families are destroyed by this.

Friendships end because of this. All of life can change in a very, very dramatic fashion when we choose to dwell on the negative.

I felt inspired to include this chapter within the book to remind you of the power of positivity in your relationship dynamics. It's time to see the good again. It's time to begin to view the connections in your life through a different lens. If you want to build strong relationships, you're going to have to start to believe that good truly exists in the relationships around you. It's a divine principle within creation. When you look for the good and believe in the good, you will always find more of the good.

One of the greatest lessons I've learned in my life, through my years of success coaching, is that there really are no bad relationships. Not really. And there are no bad people. Everyone is loved by God, and there's grace for all. So, no villains and no real enemies. It's just that some connections weren't meant for us to have.

That person you're fighting with right now isn't really your enemy or a villain. They're just someone you aren't supposed to relate to now. And that's OK. Some stories are filled with goodbyes and endings. Knowing when to say goodbye is very important where relationships are concerned. In fact, I've devoted an entire chapter within this book to the power of saying goodbye. Whether it's the breakup or the divorce or the ending of a friendship, endings exist for a reason, the same as beginnings do. But I digress. Back to the power of seeing beauty in our connections.

I can still hear it now. The song and lyrics ringing within my mind. Truthfully, it's one of my favorite songs. Not only does the song remind me of the goodness of life, but it also reminds me of the goodness of people. I know we're taught to hate others, but the truth is, there really are some good people out there. Good people still exist in the world. That is, if you can bring yourself to believe that.

The song I'm talking about is *What a Wonderful World* by Louis Armstrong. Well, at least it was Louis Armstrong responsible for making the song popular. The lyrics still inspire me. "What a Wonderful World" was written by Bob Thiele and George David Weiss. It was recorded by Louis Armstrong and released in 1967 as a single. To this day it's regarded as one of the most iconic songs of all time.

I see trees of green, red roses too

I see them bloom, for me and for you

And I think to myself

What a wonderful world

I see skies of blue, and clouds of white

The bright blessed days, dark sacred nights

And I think to myself

What a wonderful world

The colors of the rainbow so pretty in the sky

Are also on the faces of people going by

I see friends shaking hands sayin' how do you do

They're really sayin' I love you

I hear babies cry, I watch them grow

They'll learn much more than I'll never know

And I think to myself

What a wonderful world

Yes, I think to myself

What a wonderful world

Of the beautiful words, personally, I think the part that touches me most is, "The colors of the rainbow so pretty in the sky are also on the faces of people going by. I see friends shaking hands sayin' how do you do. They're really sayin' I love you." Could it be that the world really is filled with goodness? Might it be that people are, at their core, truly good? Maybe there really are no enemies – just people looking to relate to other people. Some of those people we just can't relate to or identity with. And that's okay.

When you begin to understand the true power of relatability and the power of relationship, you will begin to see the beauty of this world in a whole new light. Instead of focusing on the negative and looking for the bad in people, why not begin to see the good instead? I promise it's there if you look long enough. You'll find it if you look for it. That's how all of life works, if you really think about it.

This has a lot more to do with the power of belief and perception than it does with people. The people in the world aren't your problem. The problem, instead, is your perception of the people around you. You really have no enemies. You're just looking at the connections around you in all the wrong ways. Choosing to see the bad rather than the good. And if it really is that bad, again, you can always walk away.

Personally, I like to believe that in the very beginning when the Creator created man, He did so to show uniqueness and diversity. The creator is an artist. We find his artistic expression in all of life, each day. When God created the world, he filled it with color and with individuality. If you want to see uniqueness, simply look at the people in the world around you. We're all different, unique expressions of a beautiful and loving Creator. Truly, there's nothing more divine than uniqueness and individual expression.

There's no one on planet Earth like you. You are unique. You are fearfully and wonderfully made. It's important to remember this. But it's also important to remember that just as you are unique, so too is everyone else on planet Earth. And we're all just looking for ways to relate to each other, all looking to find where we truly fit.

Part of building stronger relationships requires that you begin to see that everyone else in the world around you is looking for the same relatability that you are. This is why I sometimes say it's better to just let other people live their lives rather than always feeling the need to control other people. Do you really, truly want to live in a world where everyone is the same as you? Don't get me wrong. I'm sure you're great, but I think that would get boring quickly.

Part of what makes life so beautiful is the uniqueness and the sense of individuality we all have. We are all aspects of a loving Creator who loves nothing more than expression. Each day, you enjoy the freedom to express yourself in any way that you choose. Well, part of having stronger relationships means that you should allow others to have that same freedom of expression. Stop trying to control others or to mold them to fit your standards. If you don't relate to someone, just move along and wish them well. Afterall, it really is a big world.

But here's where things can also get a little confusing and a little overwhelming. In a world filled with so much diversity and so much uniqueness, in a world filled with so much color, how is it truly possible to relate to anyone? How is it truly possible to find a sense of commonality when we're all so very, very different? Is it possible to even relate at all? At first glance, the answer may seem to be a resounding no. If you find yourself feeling overwhelmed in the connections of your life, it's time to start looking at your relationships in a very different way.

Just as you have feelings and emotions and desires, so too does everyone else on planet Earth. Think of it for a moment. You have your own unique interests, ideas, philosophies, and beliefs. But so too does everyone else on planet Earth. You might prefer a certain type of music, a certain type of food, or a certain drink. While others might have very different preferences. And those things are only the tip of the iceberg.

Think about beliefs for a moment. You have your beliefs. Others have theirs. Religiously, spiritually, politically, sociologically, you have your own worldview. It is a worldview that helps you to define your place in the world. But so too does everyone else on Planet Earth. And while you're busy looking to find your place to fit, so too is everyone else.

Do you really want to build stronger relationships in your life? Do you really want more quality connections than ever before? If so, it's time to begin allowing others the freedom that you want in your life. It's time to begin to allow others the same freedom to express their uniqueness and their own individuality, the same as you give yourself. This is truly a beautiful, remarkable and very, very colorful world. It's a world filled with many colorful and beautiful people.

Right now, whether you realize it or not, the reason the connections in your life feel so overwhelming or so confusing is because you've tried to change others to conform to your mold This isn't relatability. This is control. It's manipulation. It's sin.

Let's face it. Whether we would ever want to openly admit it or not, much of what we call relationship is our own desire to control others. Much of what we call love or compatibility, in fact is simply manipulation in disguise. Many times, it's our own insecurity. Sometimes it's simply our desire to get whatever we want. It's sin. It's judgment.

But we've all been guilty of it. I know I have. Wanting others to believe like me or think like me or act like me. Or wanting others to do the things that I want them to do. How easy it is to forget that we live in such a beautiful, colorful world of uniqueness and individuality. In closing this chapter, I want to encourage you to see the beauty in relationships again by learning to recognize the beauty in individuality. It's a principle within life, and a principle within the Kingdom of God. What we give to others we will receive within our own lives. What we measure to others will be measured into us. We reap what we sow.

Chapter Three

The Power of Union

There were tears in her eyes as she spoke to me, and she had the most beautiful smile upon her face. It was the look of pure joy. Pure bliss. When Amanda, a dear friend and valued client, shared with me the experience of her recent wedding day, there was nothing but joy. She lovingly and excitedly recounted the moment when, standing before her husband, she made her vows before God. "Jeremy," she said, "I'm starting to understand the power of union."

Few things illustrate the importance and the power of union quite like the vows shared before God in holy matrimony. Those vows made before God remind us of the importance of agreeing. They symbolize the true meaning of being in one accord. In many ways it's the height of relationship. At least where romantic relationship is concerned.

All too often, though, we think of Union in the terms of marriage. In fact, most often we reserve the term solely for the purpose of matrimony. We're programmed to do that. Growing up, we read fairy tales and hear stories of White Knights on horses coming to save the day. We're raised to believe in true love. What we sometimes fail to understand, though, is that in all the relationships in life, we are always making certain agreements. In every connection we have, an agreement is made.

It may not seem this way at first. In fact, at first glance, it may seem that many of our connections and most of our relationships are simply casual. Most often we never stop to think of what our relationships mean or of how those relationships are impacting us. But with every connection we make in life, we also make a conscious choice to connect. This is how friendships begin. This is how business partnerships begin. This is also how romance begins.

Some call it a feeling. Some call it a vibe. But no matter what you choose to call it in, regardless of the term you choose to use in every connection, relationally there is always an energetic exchange of some sort. In every friendship and every relationship, and in every connection, we are always in the process of exchanging energy with others. We give our energy to them. We receive their energy into ourselves. Literally every connection in life is an exchange of energy.

I wanted to include this chapter within the book for you to say it's time to begin to think a lot more carefully about the connections you're investing your energy into. Whether you've realized it or not, you've taken on the energy of a lot of people around you. And in some way, you've made an agreement with them. Although it may not be on the conscious level, and although you may not be fully aware of it, you've exchanged energy with everyone you've chosen to be in relationship with. Some of those exchanges feel very good. Others not so good.

It's time to reevaluate. To reassess. To take stock. In fact, it's time to truly notice the power of connection.

Have you ever been around someone after the very first meeting, it felt as though the life was drained from you? I sometimes like to think of these people as energy vampires. They always take, but rarely give. Then, on the opposite end of the spectrum, there are those who inspire us. There are some who, even after a single exchange, brighten our entire day. In all the connections of life, throughout every given moment, we are always exchanging energy with others.

I felt inspired to include this chapter within the book because it's very important that you begin to understand relationship from a more energetic perspective. Truly, everything is energy. Literally everything. This includes people. It includes all the connections we make in life.

Chances are, for a long, long time you've given a lot of your energy to connections that aren't truly worthy of your energy. Maybe you've even given time to people who aren't worthy of your time. A case in point would be all of those one-sided connections that always seem to be draining the life out of you. Those connections that just don't feel very good. Well, believe it or not, part of the reason it seems so draining is because you've allowed a connection to be made. In most cases, it's a connection that your soul isn't truly in agreement with.

From abusive relationships to manipulative friendships to business deals gone bad, every negative interaction with others is based solely on energetic exchange. It's not to say that they're bad people. It's not to say that they're villains or enemies. It's just to say that at the energetic level, they're not in agreement with you. And that you're not in agreement with them.

But the question begs to be asked. How often have we stayed in connections in which our souls were not truly in agreement? And how often have those connections felt like torture? Like they were just draining the life out of us. It's all too common, really.

Although I feel it's very important to understand that it isn't our place or our responsibility to change others, it is our responsibility to be more discerning of the energetic interactions we encounter each day of life. You can't change others, but you most certainly can discern energy.

And even more so, you do have a say in the connections that you choose to agree to.

By becoming more discerning of the importance of agreement where union is concerned, you and I will become much, much more selective in the people we choose to agree with. It should be noted here that you aren't designed to be friends with everyone. In fact, you aren't even designed to get close to everyone. But it truly is a very real principle, in life, as well as in the Kingdom of heaven, that in moments of relationship and in the connections we make, we are establishing certain agreements. We find this principle recounted all throughout the scriptures. Jesus himself, throughout his earthly life and ministry, taught greatly about the importance of agreeing. "If any two of you shall agree as touching anything."

This goes far, far beyond matters of faith and spirituality, though. It's much more relatable and much more practical. Literally every connection in your life is there because you are making a conscious choice to allow that connection to be there. In other words, suffice it to say you are choosing to make an agreement. And as a result, you are entering into an energetic union.

It's important to understand that not all energetic connections will serve you. In fact, many of these energetic connections are actively working against you. Again, it isn't because these people are bad people or are your enemies. It's simply because your soul isn't meant to agree with them. Most often, though, we continue to allow the connection. Most often, we never even question it.

Most often what I find throughout coaching sessions is that the single greatest reason confusion exists in relationships is because of energetic agreements gone wrong. If right now in your life you find some of these relationships you to be confusing or overwhelming or if it seems they're draining the life out of you, it's because you signed up for something you never should have signed up for in the first place. Even then, in the very beginning, your soul was speaking to you. Maybe the vibe felt off. Maybe there was just a moment of hesitancy. This is why discernment is crucial.

For a moment, I want you to think of the most significant, most important connections in your life. Think of the people that matter most. These connections represent energetic exchanges. Soul ties and soul contracts, if you will. Where many connections in life are concerned, meaning the connections we choose for ourselves, these energetic contracts are of the utmost importance. It's especially important to become more discerning of these connections.

Often when thinking of romantic relationships, we love nothing more than to consider the term soulmate. The one. That special someone. However, what we so often forget is that all through life we're making other soul contracts and creating other soul ties. We do this by allowing others to have space within our lives. We do this when we unconsciously allow energetic agreements to take place. Meaning simply, there are some connections that absolutely should not be allowed within our lives. Though it's important to love and value and honor other people, it's equally important to love and honor yourself as well. It's time to reclaim your own energy again.

It's time to become more discerning of all the connections in your life. It's time to take note of all the moments of energetic exchange. The truth is, my friend, some connections simply aren't worth your energy. Some connections are not even deserving of another single moment of your time. I'll share more on this later and even give a few helpful hints on how to properly say goodbye. However, suffice it to say, your relationships are energetic in nature. After all, that's why we call it attraction. But we not only attract romantically, but we also attract all the connections in our lives.

It's time to reassess, and it's time to take stock. If certain relationships and connections within your life seem to be draining the life energy out of you, it's time to reevaluate what you've agreed to. The agreement that you are so agreed to, that is. Allow me to say it in another way that's perhaps even more practical and more relatable. All throughout life, in any given day, you're going to encounter many, many, many people. However, not all these people deserve a place within your energetic field. In fact, quite simply, most do not. It's time you recognize that.

All throughout life, you and I are giving our energy to something or to someone. We do this with every passing conversation, in every moment with people. All throughout the day, you and I are being constantly bombarded with energetic exchanges. We protect ourselves more when we learn to use the power of discernment within our lives. The truth is you can always read people. It doesn't even take a strong prophetic gifting. You can always tell the energy of someone by the way you feel. By becoming more discerning of this energetic exchange, you will become much more selective of the relationships you choose to give your life to.

Another, perhaps even better, way to say this is to say it's time to take note of all the connections in your life. Beyond romantic connections, beyond friendships, beyond partnerships, beyond business dealings, you and I constantly meet many, many other people. You have been given the power to determine how far into your life they are allowed to move. And only you can decide that. Suffice it to say, you've been given a very divine power in your selection of your connections. It's time to use that power to your advantage. It's time to begin to choose more wisely.

Chapter Four

Who's In Your Corner?

You don't need more relationships in your life. You need quality relationships. Allow me to say it another way. You don't need more people. You need the right people.

Whether you've ever taken the time to realize it or not, all your success in life will be determined by the people you choose to surround yourself with. Now, that's not to say that others are going to be responsible for your success in life. However, that you can either make or break your destiny based on the people you choose to allow into your inner circle. Not everyone deserves a seat at your table. Part of success comes from learning who to allow into your life.

When Michael first reached out to me and contacted the offices of Identity Network to schedule a life coaching session, he was three years into being the owner of a successful architecture firm. Having an interest in architectural design for as long as he could remember, it was the career he had always dreamed of. The first year seemed like a dream. The second year seemed even better. But at the end of the second year, nearing the third year, trouble began to arise as the firm began to lose high-paying clients. To make matters worse, Michael's business partner, Anthony, began contemplating leaving also.

Allow me to share a little more of the history. The reason that Michael was even able to successfully launch his firm was because of an investment from Anthony. Michael had been an up-and-coming designer in another firm when he caught the eye of Anthony. Anthony, a millionaire investor, wanted to support the up-and-coming designer in a new venture. In the beginning, it seemed like a business connection made in Heaven. Michael had big dreams and big vision and very big ideas. And Anthony had more than enough money to make those dreams a reality. It seemed the perfect business partnership. Well, that is, until things began to go south.

"I just can't be a part of this any longer," Anthony said. "I have no choice but to pull funding." Michael was devastated. The one person who had always believed in his dream seemed to be taking a step back. Of course, in the world of business, decisions like this are made daily. And truthfully, investors must protect their investments. It isn't personal, it's just business.

But for Michael, it felt like a sense of betrayal. Honestly, to a certain extent, it was. From

Michael's perspective, the man who had always been there, who had always believed in the vision, was running away when he needed the support most. I share this story in the beginning of this chapter to say simply, you need to become more selective in who you choose to allow in your corner. Money will always come and go. Loyalty, though, is very, very hard to find.

So here at the very beginning of this chapter, I'd like to ask you a very real question. Who's in your corner? When you think to the connections and the relationships in your life, who are the connections that really have your back? Chances are though you may have many relationships, only a few fit that criteria. Perhaps it's only one. Chances are, if you were to be honest, there may not even be a single person. Maybe for you, it seems you've always had to do it alone.

One thing that I found within my own life and even in my own business ventures, is that when the going gets rough, you're going to realize who your true friends are. In fact, it's always in moments of adversity, it seems, when real connections begin to make themselves known. Lasting connections. Strong relationships. The people that matter most.

True colors are always revealed, most in moments of adversity. Moments of tribulation. Times of testing and hardship. In times of hardship, we not only see what we're made of, but we also see the true colors of those around us. I would advise you, my friend, pay close attention. When things get hard, you're going to see the true colors of those closest to you. In fact, it's when things get most difficult that most people will decide to run, leaving you to face the giant alone. In these moments, thank them for their time and let them go. With friends like that, who needs enemies?

I sense you can relate in some way. Chances are you've encountered this many times in your own life. I sense you're a giver. You genuinely care. Chances are, for most of your life, you've been the person to give most. Whenever someone was in need, you were always there. But when you needed others most, chances are, you were left alone. Does that feel relatable to you?

My friend, please hear me and understand when I say that few things in existence will ever drain the life out of you like one-sided connections will. Not only will they drain the life of you, but they will destroy your dream and your destiny. Don't allow it to happen. You're familiar with these one-sided connections in your own life I'm sure. The connections who always seem to take when it benefits them. Who are always there when it serves them. Other times, they're nowhere to be found.

As much as it pains me to say and as bitter a bill as it may seem to swallow, there are people in your life who do not truly value you. They only value what you bring to them. They only value what you represent to them. In the example of Michael and Anthony, although both mutually benefited from the connection for a season, when times got rough, true colors were revealed. I also share this to say don't expect everyone to believe in your dreams the way you do. After all, they are your dreams.

My friend, allow me to share with you one of the most powerful spiritual principles I've learned within my own life. Not everyone is going to have your back. Well, at least the way you expect them to. It's not because they're bad people, or your enemies, or some villain, mind you. It's that in most instances, it's every man for himself. Whether right or wrong, that's just the way life works sometimes. It's time for you to become more discerning of who's in your corner. Your success will depend on that.

If you want to truly build stronger relationships, you're going to have to become more selective in who you allow into your corner. It's all too common. I see it in marriages, in friendships and in business partnerships. At the end of the day, success always stems, in part, from the people we surround ourselves with. Why is the inner circle truly important? Because it can either help build you or it can destroy you.

For a moment, think of the world of professional boxing. Every prized fighter has someone dependable in his corner. Whether it's words of encouragement and inspiration, clear direction or insight, insight on strategy, or just a refreshing drink of water when needed most, the person in the corner serves a purpose. You need people in your life who can see your vision as clearly as you do. And most of all, who are willing to support it. Especially when times get rough. Because believe me, they will.

And we find this principle illustrated all throughout the scriptures, in fact. We find the power of agreement. We find the power of partnership. And also, we see what happens when there's a Judas in the mix. Much like the Scriptures remind us, a little leaven can ruin the entire loaf.

My hope and prayer for you, my friend, is that in all your relationships you choose quality over all else. In fact, it's time to become a lot more selective of who you allow into your corner. By this I mean to say your inner circle matters. In fact, it matters greatly. Your success in many ways is directly related to who you choose to surround yourself with. And in this I'm speaking of more than simple partnerships.

It should also be noted, however, that although not everyone will always be in your corner, not everyone is supposed to be. Not everyone will believe in your dream. And that's OK. Not everyone is supposed to. They have dreams of their own. Don't take it personally.

But in marriage, in friendship and in partnership, you need the assurance that your partner is in your corner. We all need that assurance at times. When hard times and times of struggle come, and rest assured they will, you need to know that you're not alone. Jesus himself said that in this world there will always be times of trouble. Not only is it alright to be selective of who you allow in your corner, it's imperative.

One of the most important aspects of building stronger relationships is being selective of who you allow into your corner. Because when the going gets rough, you'll need them. You'll need the support and validation. Often, you'll need the inspiration that comes from knowing someone is on your team. Whether you've realized it or not, throughout your entire life you've been assembling a team. A team of connections.

In case you have yet to notice, life has a funny way of revealing people's true motives and intentions. Although discernment is important, most often it doesn't take a very strong prophetic gifting to see someone's true colors. True colors always come to the surface. Hidden motives are always revealed. You can't hide who you truly are, and the truth will always find you. It's the same for all of us in life.

Has it ever felt that you were alone in a crowded room? That no matter the people around you, you've always felt alone? If so, I would humbly suggest it's time to become more selective of who you choose to be in your corner. Just because there are many people on your field, it doesn't necessarily mean that these people are on your team. It's time you realize that. In fact, you'll save yourself a great deal of heartache by seeing it now. And yes, the team that you are assembling for your life truly, truly matters. Although it's not good to be alone, being alone is often far better than being in partnership with someone who doesn't truly believe in you.

If you think back to some of the most difficult moments of your life, those times when it seemed that you were about to lose it all, the reason you made it through, most often, was because someone was in your corner. Maybe it was the simple text from a friend. Perhaps it was the family member offering encouragement or a word of advice. Maybe it was even the coworker. I would dare to suggest, however, that in the lowest moments of your life, when you needed hope most, someone was there. Learn to be more discerning. Pay attention to these people. Chances are you'll need them again.

One of the most beautiful things about life on planet Earth is the power of oneness and interconnectedness. Just as you need others to support your dreams, others also need you. All too often the truth is we're a little self-centered when it comes to our own goals, dreams and visions. It's easy to become self-absorbed when you're focused on your dreams. But it simply must be asked, are you supporting the dreams of others also? Are you contributing to the vision of those around you? Are you offering support? If not, don't be surprised if you find yourself all alone when the going gets rough.

All throughout life you are assembling a team of players, and the players matter greatly. It's time to become much more discerning than ever before. Much more selective. By choosing who you allow into your corner, you are setting yourself up for a greater measure of success. And in the process, chances are you're also making a lifelong connection.

Chapter Five

Building Trust

Five years ago, when Cassie reached out to the offices of Identity Network to inquire about her prophetic word for her love life, she had questions about romance. The thought of love was at the top of her mind. No matter what she did, it seemed she would never find the right person. She asked, "What am I doing wrong?" If you now find yourself in the search for true and lasting love, chances are you can relate.

It's a great, big and beautiful world out there. It's a world filled with uniqueness, diversity, and many, many interesting characters. It's filled with so many people, in fact, that sometimes the search for the right ones can seem a little overwhelming. For Cassie and her search for love, it wasn't that there weren't people for her, it was that it seemed there were far too many people to choose from. Often, I find this issue arise when coaching clients looking for romance. We live in a world filled with many, many options. That is a beautiful thing. But let's face it, it can seem a little overwhelming at times.

I could sense the genuine feeling of despair in her voice. It was obvious. After a string of unsuccessful meetings, she found herself reeling in the pain of loneliness. But as I listened more closely, the real reason for the despair began to reveal itself. It was difficult for her to trust. I wanted to include this chapter on the topic of trust because I sense in some way you can relate. If in life you find that it's difficult to trust other people, chances are somewhere along the way you were hurt. Cassie, like so many of us, had been hurt.

Few things in existence hurt relationships quite like the betrayal of trust. Most often, the harsh truth is there's no coming back from it. Once trust has been jeopardized, it's difficult to find trust again. Chances are you can relate to this fact. But for a moment, let's put aside the spirituality and look at this in a much more practical and more relatable and personal way. Nothing hurts in life more than betrayal. Betrayal hurts us. It shakes us to the core of who we are.

"I just didn't think I could trust him", Cassie said. Chances are, she was probably right. She recounted to me that when she had first met Brian, although there was immediate attraction, there were lies which were obvious even at the very beginning. She didn't think much of it at first. It seemed insignificant at the time. Have you ever stopped to think of how much heartbreak we allow into our own lives simply because we often choose to ignore the still small voice? Most often there are always red flags. Usually, we simply choose to ignore them.

It's not always easy to trust other people. Especially when you've been hurt, and your trust has been betrayed. However, I wanted to include for you this chapter to say that, believe it or not, there are still very good people left on planet Earth. And surprisingly, maybe even miraculously, perhaps, there are still people who can truly be trusted. Be discerning. But don't allow your past pain to keep you from experiencing all that life has to offer. I think what I truly mean to say is don't be afraid to make new connections because of past pains. There's still a great big world ready to be experienced and enjoyed. And there are still many valuable relationships to be made.

Each relationship is personal and unique. No two are ever the same. In every relationship you will ever make on planet Earth, you must find the fit that works best for you. But trust, however, will always be an important factor. And rightfully so. In marriage, in partnership, in friendship and even in business dealings, trust is essential.

Let's make one thing perfectly clear here and now, just to get it out of the way. There is never any good excuse for a lie. In fact, any reasoning you ever give for a lie would be just that, nothing more than an excuse. When we lie, no matter the justification, we create more heartbreak for ourselves in the end. It's a law within creation. Everything in existence operates by truth and transparency. There are no gray areas where truth is concerned.

But rather than dwelling on past hurts in moments of betrayal, I want to ask you another question. Are you yourself trustworthy? Are you a person of trust and integrity? Or do you justify lies within your life? Most often in life, our relationships mirror who we truly are. Surprisingly, most often, the reason we see the darkness in others so clearly is because we possess that same darkness within ourselves. Nothing kills a strong relationship quite like hypocrisy. Many times, in relationships, though we would never dare to admit it openly, we judge others for the same things that we ourselves continue to do. This, again, is one of those uncomfortable mirror moments.

I'm not saying this to you in any way diminish the past or to negate your own traumatic moments of betrayal. I'm not even saying this to in any way condone the lies that you've endured. What I am saying, however, is that you should never use your own painful moments from the past as ways to justify your own lack of integrity. On planet Earth, there are many people who do not value integrity. But still, there are many who do. If trust and integrity are important to you, walk in integrity regardless. When you do, I promise you, life has a way of sending to you the relationships and connections that will mirror that integrity.

For a moment, let's return to the example of Cassie. Throughout countless relationships in the past, Cassie had been lied to and betrayed. It seemed that no one could be trusted. Unsurprisingly, this made her enter every new connection and potential relationships with a sense of suspicion. Her past continued to haunt her. As a result, even when meeting genuine people, she remained highly suspicious. Who could blame her? But the purpose of this chapter isn't to victim shame. It's to say simply that despite traumatic moments, in times of betrayal in her past, Cassie was still being given a choice. Would she remain open to new potential connections? Or would she allow the traumatic moments of her past and times of hurt to define her? And most importantly, would she herself continue to be a person of integrity?

You see, when it comes to building strong relationships, we're all being given a choice each day. It's really a beautiful thing if you truly think about it. Day after day on Planet Earth, you and I are being given the opportunity to decide who we will allow into our lives. Most often, we make wise choices. Other times, there are those times we will regret the decisions we've made. In case you have yet to notice it yet the truth always has a way of coming to the surface. What's done in the darkness will always come to light.

Where we so often begin to make a mess of things, however, is when we place expectations on others, expecting them to possess qualities that we ourselves refuse to possess. Or when we hypocritically blame others for doing the very same things that we ourselves are doing. Again, our relationships have a way of mirroring who we are. Sometimes I like to think of relationships as the sort of universal mirror, a tool of Heaven by which to sometimes see the changes that we need to make within our own lives. My advice to Cassie was simple. Continue to be a person of integrity and the universe will send you exactly what you desire.

The topic of trust is such an important topic. In fact, I've written an entire book on the subject. As I felt the inspiration to write this book, I wanted to include this chapter to say that trust is important in every type of connection we have in life on planet Earth. From romantic relationships to friendship to business partnerships, to even the familial connections we have with family members, trust matters. However, if in life it seems you can't find someone trustworthy, my advice would be, continue to walk in integrity regardless. I promise you; Heaven is noticing and the universe is taking notes.

I know right now it may not seem like it. But there are still many wonderful people on planet Earth who value trust. Still, for many people, the issue of trust is important. There are still people who value integrity also. I share this to say simply don't allow the pains of your past to cause you to judge others before giving them a chance. Chances are you've been hurt and betrayed through lies in your past. Don't allow these painful moments from your past to cause you to become jaded where relationships are concerned. Just as you deserve grace, give grace to others. And if it feels the trust cannot be restored, simply walk away.

Chances are, where relationships are concerned, you've been hurt many times in your past. Chances are, it seems, you've been betrayed more times than you could even count. But where all those new potential relationships and new connections are concerned, it's no one else's responsibility to atone for the sins of the people in your past. When making new connections, be open. And if you want to find a new relationship connection based in trust, remain a person of integrity. The universe will send to us exactly what we desire. That is, if we remove hypocrisy. So, do you really want to know the best way to build a strong relationship based in trust? The answer is simple. Decide that you yourself will be a person of integrity. Be a person who can be trusted.

Chapter Six

A Return to Loyalty

"You can do anything, but never go against the family." This immortal line from Francis Ford Coppola's blockbuster film *The Godfather* reveals the power of loyalty. But in case you have yet to notice, loyalty isn't merely a trait reserved for members of the mafia. Loyalty is a very important quality that we're all looking for in our connections in life. You need people in your corner, but the truth is, not everyone's going to cut it. You need people that you can count on. You need people that are going to be loyal to your vision. Loyalty matters.

It's dangerous to overlook the quality of loyalty. In fact, it can be deadly. It's important that you surround yourself in life with people who not only support your dream and your vision, but people who are going to be loyal to it. In life, has it ever felt like you've been unequally yoked with others? Has it felt that no matter what you've tried, you've just never seemed to find someone who supports you fully? It's time to rethink the power of loyalty. In literally every connection you make in life on planet Earth in some way, shape, form or capacity, the topic of loyalty is going to come into question. It's important, even though we don't realize it. Many times, it just remains an unspoken thing. Often, we never bring it up in conversation. However, deep down at the core, we all seem to know that we want people on our side.

In case you have yet to realize it or not, life on planet Earth is filled with many wonderful, interesting and remarkable people. These people, these characters within your life, have a role to play. However, so too do you have a role to play as well. As you've realized by now, it's important to not only have connections in your life, but it's also important to make the right connections. The people who you choose to allow into your circle matter greatly. Much of your success in life will be determined by who you allow into your circle. One of the greatest, most important attributes concerning relationships is that of loyalty. When making relationships of any kind, loyalty will matter greatly.

It's something I hear about all too often when coaching clients concerning love and relationships. It seems most often the topic of loyalty comes up most when we're discussing topics of romance. The truth is, however, loyalty takes on many forms and many different types of relationships. Romantic relationships are merely one of many. Even in friendships and business partnerships, and in platonic connections of all manner, the topic of loyalty matters. You not only need people in your life who are in your corner, you need people who are loyal to you and to your vision. There's a lot to be said about being on the same page.

Chances are, when you hear the topic of loyalty come up in conversation, your mind drifts to moments of heartbreak, heartache, or times of betrayal. There again, chances are you think of the concept of loyalty where romantic relationships are concerned. However, I would dare to suggest that there have also been moments in life in which your friendships have suffered due to a lack of loyalty. Perhaps at times, even in business, there were moments in which confusion arose due to a lack of loyalty. Again, it simply cannot be stressed enough that where connections are concerned, loyalty matters.

I felt inspired to include this chapter within the book to say that where loyalty is concerned, it's not only important that you find loyal people, but it's important that you yourself have a better understanding of what it truly means to be loyal. To have friends, we must show ourselves friendly. However, the same could be said for loyalty. If you're looking for loyalty in your life, you need to look in the mirror. Are you yourself a person who values loyalty? It's an important question to consider. After all, remember, your relationships are always ways going to mirror your own life.

When the going gets rough, and it will in life, you're going to need someone around you that's going to not only have your back, but someone who's going to also have your best interests at heart. These connections aren't always easy to find. But when they are found, they should be treasured at all cost. Surprisingly, the Scriptures have much to say about the power of loyalty. Loyalty, not only in our dealings with God, but also loyalty in our dealings with each other.

He who pursues righteousness and loyalty finds life, righteousness, and honor. Proverbs 21:21

There are friends who destroy each other, but a real friend sticks closer than a brother. Proverbs 18:24

There is no greater love than to lay down one's life for one's friends. John 15:13

I'm giving you a new commandment. Love each other in the same way that I have loved you. Everyone will know that you are my disciples because of your love for each other. John 13:34-35

A friend always loves and a brother is born for time of adversity. Proverbs 17:17

Love bears all things, believes all things, hopes all things, endures all things. First Corinthians 13:7.

A man of many companions may come to ruin, but there is a friend who stays closer than a brother. Proverbs 18:24

Many a man proclaims his loving devotion, but who can find a trustworthy man? Proverbs 20:6

In the above referenced Scripture verses, we find that loyalty seems to be very difficult to find. It's a very rare treasure. These passages within the scripture revealed the power of loyalty not only in our connection to God and faith, but also, just as equally important, our connection to other people. When the going gets rough and it will happen, you need someone to stand by you. Someone you can trust. Could it be that when we talk about the, the topic of loyalty, what we're referring to is a deeper level of trust? According to the scriptures, it would seem so.

In the Book of Proverbs, we find that a friend loves at all times and brothers are born in times of adversity. If you think back over the course of your life, think to many of the most difficult moments you've encountered. I think it would be easy to assume it was in those painful moments, those moments of trial and testing, that you found out who your true friends really were. Something about adversity, it reveals true intention. Times of testing and times of trial in life remind us of those most loyal to us?

But also, within the Scriptures we seem to be reminded that loyalty doesn't come easily. That it comes at a great cost. It's easy to stand by someone when everything's going according to plan. But when the going gets rough, do you have what it takes to stay close to those you love most? This is where true loyalty is confirmed. True loyalty is confirmed most in times of adversity and in times of hardship. It's easy to have friends when you're successful and when you're on the mountaintop. Anyone can make friends in those conditions. However, in times of adversity, we seem to find most those who are truly sincere in their loyalty to us. I would dare to suggest that in your most difficult moments, those painful moments of the past, it was in those times that you realized who your true friends were. For a moment, I'd like for you to think about those moments.

Allow me to share with you one of the most powerful, most revolutionary revelations I've received within my own life. If you receive this truth, I promise it's going to help you and save you an awful lot of heartache. Are you ready? Well, here goes. Not all friends are created equal. Read that again.

As you think back to some of the most difficult, most painful moments of your life, those times in which it felt as though the rug was swept from underneath your feet, it was in those times that you connected with certain people. Maybe it was the trusted confidant who listened to you. Maybe it was the friend who sent a text to say I'm thinking of you and I'm here. Perhaps when going through a painful divorce in the past, or maybe suffering the loss of a career, it was the friend who always seemed to stand by your side, to encourage you, to motivate you and to inspire you. Truth is, when you think back to some of the most difficult moments of your life, in those moments, you're also going to find memories of certain people. But not all these people were created equally. Some stayed close. Others even closer. Some remained. Chances are some are still by your side today.

You see, when we're talking about the topic of loyalty, what we're in essence truly talking about is staying power. The power to remain loyal and stand by one's side even in times of adversity.

This is where true loyalty will always be tested. In case you have yet to notice, life is filled with many ups and downs. But for some reason, it always seems to be that it's in the times when we're down that we need loyalty the most. All those down times in life, those times remind of what true loyalty means.

Loyalty doesn't mean that everything's always going to go according to plan. It doesn't mean that there won't be difficult moments at times. In fact, having people loyal to you doesn't even mean that you won't have moments in life in which things aren't going to be very, very turbulent. In other words, loyalty doesn't guarantee smooth connections and smooth relationships to other people. What loyalty does remind us of, though, however, is that we'll never truly be alone. It reminds us that even when someone walks away, they'll ultimately return. That's what loyalty does. It stays.

In all of life on planet Earth, in romantic connections and business dealings and partnerships and even platonic connections with friendships, there's going to be a certain sense of loyalty that will always come into play. In some connections to people, loyalty will be apparent in the very beginning. For some connections made, it will be obvious very early on that there is no true sense of loyalty. However, for most connections in life, we learn loyalty through times of adversity. And in most instances in life, it's only in the moments of trial and testing that we see what loyalty truly means. Most often, it's only then, in moments of hardship that we see what loyalty is to those closest to us. Times of trial and times of tribulation reveal the most loyal.

As I said in the very beginning of this book, it's not enough to have connections in life and make relationships. You need the right relationships.

You need quality relationships, quality connections. Of all the qualities, however, loyalty is one of the most important. Much of your success in life will be determined by who you're loyal to. Remember and keep in mind, loyalty isn't a one-way St.

Are you ready for a bitter pill swallow? Are you ready to take a long, hard look in the mirror? How often have you expected loyalty from someone within your life, the entire time you haven't yourself been loyal? Remember, relationships in your life will always mirror your true self. This is the universal law of attraction. We reap what we sow. If you find yourself surrounded by people who don't value loyalty, chances are it's a very good indicator that you yourself haven't prioritized loyalty to others in your own life. In other words, have you demanded loyalty from people while not being loyal yourself? Just as the Scriptures remind us that to have friends, we must show ourselves friendly, well, the same can be said of loyalty. If you expect loyalty from others, you yourself must become more loyal. In your dealings with others, in all matters of relationships and life on planet Earth, your sense of loyalty will matter greatly.

However, chances are even as you read these words, when you think back some of those most difficult moments in your life, many times it may seem as though you were alone. Chances are, when you think back, there's the initial feeling that no one was there by your side. Maybe you truly were alone. Maybe it seems as you look back that aside from God and the power of the Holy Spirit, you were left to fend all for yourself in times of adversity. If this seems to be the case, however, I urge you to not become jaded. Don't become cynical. I would urge you to continue living a life of loyalty. Continue being your true self. When you do, I promise you the universe will send to you loyal connections and loyal companions.

I began this chapter with very powerful line from Francis Ford Coppola's blockbuster hit *The Godfather*. "You can do anything, but never go against the family." These words of Don Vito Corleone, portrayed by Marlon Brando in the film, reveal the power of loyalty. Well, in life on planet Earth, although we're not a mob or a mafia, we really are a family, if you truly think about it. We're all in this together. As cliche as it may seem at first glance, our connections to people determine the outcome of our lives. And just as life is filled with many wonderful, interesting, unique characters, these characters play a very important role in the outcomes we experience. It's time to rethink the topic of loyalty. But it's not enough to place an expectation of loyalty onto other people or the connections around you. It's time to look in the mirror. If you expect loyalty from others, you yourself must begin to value loyalty within your own life. To have loyalty, you must become loyal.

Chapter Seven

The Seeds of Friendship

In the previous chapter, I shared with you the importance of loyalty. Through several powerful, poignant scriptures, we realized the power of loyalty in connections and in life. Well, in case you didn't notice it, most of those scriptures dealt also with the topic of friendship. If you're going to begin to build better, stronger relationships in life, not only is it important to recognize the connections you make, but you need to reevaluate the topic of friendship as well. The Scriptures remind us that to have friends we must show ourselves friendly. But is it enough to be a friendly person? If so, why is it that sometimes we seem to be so alone in life?

I wanted to include this chapter within the book to remind you of the importance of friendship. Now, I'll admit, on the surface of things, at first glance the topic of friendship may seem quite trivial. But for a moment, let's put aside the spirituality and look at friendship in a more practical, more relatable way. What does friendship, true friendship that is, look like in life on planet Earth? How do we truly define friendship? Perhaps a better, even more appropriate question would be how do we define the term "friend?"

Is a friend, simply someone you text on occasion? Is a friend a person you go to the movies with or enjoy the nice dinner with during your evening out? Is a friend someone you can share your deepest burning questions with? Or is friendship altogether something entirely different? I suppose what I mean to ask is, what does friendship look like to you? That's really the important question, if you truly think about it. Only you can answer that question for yourself.

But here at the very beginning, I feel it is important and necessary even to ask that question. Because in case you have yet to realize it or not, the way in which you answer that question has really determined the connections you've already made in life on planet Earth. Does it feel as though you have no friends? Does life feel lonely for you even now? Well, if so, I would respectfully ask, how are you choosing to define the term friend? And are you yourself, within your own life, being the type of friend you want to attract into your life? Remember, it simply can't be stressed enough that your connections in life will always mirror you. You're going to receive what you're putting out into the world. As the Scriptures remind us, what we measure out to others ultimately will be measured back to us.

Personally, I feel it's important to address something right here at the very beginning of this chapter. Just as life isn't always perfect, and just as it always doesn't go according to plan, there will always be moments of trial and testing, even where our friendships are concerned. The arguments will happen. The moments of disagreement will arise. There will be more than a few tense moments. But it's in these moments that we're going to recognize what true friendship really means. And through it all, we're going to learn a lot more about ourselves in the process. That's how life really works, if you truly think about it. There are always so many lessons to be learned.

But just as there is no perfect romantic relationship and no perfect business dealing, there really is no perfect friendship either. Think of that one friend within your life who just seems to drive you crazy. Chances are, as you think, to some of the people in your inner circle, there's always one person who comes to mind who just never seems to quite relate. At first glance, when you think of this person, this is typically the person who always seems to disagree with you. Just when you have your heart set on enjoying the dinner and you're in your favorite restaurant, this is the friend who always chooses something else. No, let's go here instead, they say. Typically, this one person is also the friend who when you ask about relationship or dating advice, they always seem to say you're doing it all wrong. Most often, this is also the person who says you can do better.

I think it's human nature to casually dismiss most of these people. Often at first glance, we say to ourselves this person isn't really a true friend. Most often we even go as far as to say I don't even really need that friendship within my life. We do this most often, I think, because we love to always be right. We love to always surround ourselves with people who agree with us. It's human nature, really. We live lives of confirmation bias. When someone begins to disagree with us, we often think that they are no longer a friend, but rather an enemy.

But what I find so interesting and so fascinating about these connections with certain individuals is that it's often the lessons we learn most that we find from our connections with these people. I would dare say that chances are when you think of that one friendship connection that just seems to drive you crazy, who just seems to always disagree with you, there have been moments of learning, all in part because of that connection. What I mean to say is that sometimes we learn most from the people who disagree with us. In life, we need to be challenged. We need to be confronted. And as much as we may hate to admit it, sometimes we also need to be disagreed with.

I wanted to include this chapter in the book because I think it's very important that we begin to redefine and reassess what true friendship really looks like. You don't need yes man around you. Someone to always just agree with every decision you make? No. Instead, you deserve to be challenged, and you need that. We all do. We need someone to play devil's advocate at times. Most often in life, it isn't that these moments of conflict Arised in friendships or connections with people. Most often, it's that these moments of conflict arise to teach us a valuable lesson about ourselves. Remember and keep in mind, we're all learning. We learn most through relationships.

I have a friend and client who recently shared with me just how much his life changed the moment a new coworker arrived in the office. John, my friend said to me "Jeremy, it was like a nightmare." This person seemed to be nothing but trouble from the very beginning. Do you have a few coworkers like that in your office? Chances are you do.

John shared with me that from the moment Brendan was first hired on, everything seemed to be so much more stressful. Unlike others in the office, Brenda never quite fit in. He didn't have the same conversations as the other friends. His hobbies, his interests, were different. And whenever John shared an idea with management, it seemed that Brendan opposed him at every single front. Brendan would often say, "John, that's a great idea, but what if we tried this instead?" For most of the workers who had been in the office were quite some time Brendan, the new addition seemed like nothing but a nightmare.

Though, this is how some of our most important connections in life will always seem at first glance. Usually, it's going to be the coworker you disagree with. Sometimes it's going to be the friend who opposes you in every turn. Most often, some of the most important connections in your life, whether romantically, professionally, or in business dealings, will be the connection that always seems to challenge you the most. Well, this is where John found himself in his dealings with the new coworker Brendan. Can you relate in some way?

Now to the natural, untrained eye, at first glance, it may seem that Brendan was nothing but a troublemaker. It may seem that his goal was to undermine all of John's ideas. But this wasn't really the case. Not really. You see, my friend, part of having better, stronger relationships is going to demand that you begin to discern friendships in a more appropriate way. You're going to have to look a little deeper. You're going to have to begin to look beneath the surface level of things.

So, what was really happening in the office? More appropriately and more important question to ask was what was really happening energetically. If everything happens for a reason, and if all things are being made to work for our good, well, what role exactly was Brendan there to serve? Could it be that even Brendan was part of God's plan for John's life? Absolutely.

You see, what John ultimately admitted to me was that despite the moments of what seemed so stressful. At the end of the day, one of his greatest teachers was Brendan. This is how John shared it with me. "Jeremy. I hated him at first. At first, I thought he was nothing but a troublemaker. But I have to say, his ideas challenged me and inspired me to be better at my own job. The truth is, I've learned a lot from Brendan."

And there you have it. What real, genuine friendship connections sometimes look like. Many times, true friendship looks like a challenge in the very beginning. It looks like something that doesn't really make much sense. Sometimes true friendship even looks like a moment of conflict. What I personally find so interesting, and so remarkably wonderful, however, is that it's in these moments of conflict that we see the value of true friendship within our lives. Just as friendships and life are meant to make us feel good, friendships are also divinely designed to cause us to grow. In other words, as controversial as such a statement might seem, if your friendships aren't challenging you and inspiring you to be better, are those true friendships? And are those connections you really need within your life? It's time to rethink the meaning of friendship.

As I'm writing this, my mind drifts back to thoughts of the early church. In the very beginning in Jerusalem, the Scriptures remind us that they were all together in one accord. That's when miracles happened. You're familiar with this passage of Scripture, I'm sure. For so long we've been told about friendship in this way, and we've been led to believe that friendship means we're all together in one accord. But what does it really mean to truly be in one accord? Sometimes I think we miss it.

So often when we think about the topic of friendship, what we're wanting is someone to be exactly like us. Someone to always go along with exactly what we say. But what's challenging about that? Do those connections really cause us to grow? Do they inspire us? You see, sometimes in life we view friendships in a very selfish way. We want people to agree with us, to inspire us, to support us. But most often in life, it's the challenges that we face in our dealings with people that cause us to learn most about ourselves. Friendships, true friendships, that is, are divine in this way. It's part of a divine design.

They're created to cause us to grow. Personal growth comes most through moments of adversity and in times of challenge.

You see, for my friend John, although it may have seemed at first that Brendan was nothing but trouble, it was through the connection to Brendan that John found some of his greatest inspiration in the office. In fact, some of John's greatest ideas came from inspiration from Brendan. So, looks can be deceiving at times. Although to most in the office it seemed that Brennan was nothing but a troublemaker, the reality was Brendan was divinely designed and divinely strategically placed within the office to actually cause growth. When we begin to look at all our connections in life in this way, we see that everything is part of a beautiful design.

Believe it or not, everything's really going according to plan. Even when it may not seem like that at first glance. When we talk about friendship, what we sometimes think, selfishly, is that we need people who are just like us. Well, that's simply not the case, my friend. And it's not true. You are unique. Your individual. There's no one else on planet Earth just like you. However, the same could be said of every other person on planet Earth also. I sometimes like to think that the topic of friendship reminds us of the beauty of diversity.

This is what we find in operation in the early church. When the Scriptures speak of being in one accord, what does that truly mean? Does it mean that everyone was identical? Certainly not. We're also very, very different.

Can I let you in on a little secret? The world doesn't need another version of you. One of you is more than enough. Friendships aren't meant to me. To seem identical to you. Friendships are meant to teach you. So, let's look back at the early church for a moment.

We sometimes think when thinking back to the early church and the early apostles that were there in Jerusalem, that everyone just always seemed to get along. We sometimes fantasize it and romanticize it in very unrealistic ways. We think that it was such a magical time that they were also very, very different from how we are today. But it just isn't the case. Diversity is beautiful as it is will always bring moments of tension in a few moments of conflict. But conflict is necessary for growth. Most of all, conflict is necessary to cause us to see the truth of the importance of connections.

We love to think of the ideas of the apostles being in one accord, as if they were all just always. In agreement. We sometimes forget that there were moments of very heated debate in the early church. When Peter received the vision atop the rooftop of Cornelius to take the gospel to the Gentiles, it seemed like such a blasphemous idea.

The rest of the church just didn't suddenly go along with the idea. No. Instead, it caused a moment of conflict. The apostles had to learn to reason together. And then when Saul of Tarsus, after his conversion on the road to Damascus, became the apostle Paul, well, that was another matter entirely. Not only did it seem very heated, but it seemed more like all-out war. Could this man even be termed an apostle at all? There were moments of contention in which Peter the Apostle vehemently confronted Paul. We sometimes forget about these things.

Suffice it to say, true friendships look a lot different than what we sometimes think or feel or imagine. It's not always sunshine and rainbows where friendships are concerned. But believe it or not, this is actually a very, very good thing. What I mean to say is that on the surface of things, friendships may sometimes seem very challenging. It's not always going to be easy to be a friend. And let's face it, it's not always easy to be friendly.

You see, my friend, being in one accord doesn't mean you won't to have moments of opposition. It doesn't mean that there won't be times of great tension, sometimes even strife. Friendships remind us that even in times of adversity, we're always learning. Friendships serve a purpose. They're there to teach us. And in many ways, they're also there to remind us that if we're going to have true friends, we have to ourselves be friendly. One thing I find within my own life, and I see confirmed time and time again, is that once you begin to focus on the good, you will in turn see more of the good. When you look for the good in others, you will ultimately find that goodness.

Chapter Eight

The Power of Openness

Genuineness. Loyalty. Trust. All qualities that make for strong relationships. By now you've learned that in order to have these things, you're going to have to begin to exude them, or in your own life. That you're going to have to be the very things you claim you want in other people. Change, if you truly think about it, always begins within us first.

But I've chosen to include here, toward the end of the book, what I believe to be one of the greatest, greatest principles concerning building strong relationships. It's what I find to be one of the most overlooked qualities of all. It's one of the qualities that we never really think about. However, it's also one of the qualities that's perhaps most important. It's vulnerability.

The reason you're even now holding this book within your hands is because at some core level, you seem to want better, stronger relationships in your life. Better, more meaningful connections in all manner. First, I want to commend you for your search. As you realize by now, the connections that we make with other people matter greatly. But you don't need more friends and more connections. No. Instead you need the right friends and the right connections. Unique connections of quality and of substance.

Unfortunately, all too often in our search for new connections and for meaningful relationships, we sometimes dismiss or casually disregard the power that comes from being gentle. If you think about it, it's not difficult to understand why though. And truthfully, it's not always our fault.

As the old saying goes, sometimes it's live. Sometimes in life, the hardest thing you'll ever find is being yourself. The hardest thing you'll ever do is be who you truly are. In order to position yourself to receive better, stronger relationships in your life, you're going to have to be genuine. In other words, you're going to have to take off the mask you've been wearing for far too long. It's time to think of the power of vulnerability.

We live in such a celebrity driven culture. So much so, in fact, that the idea of celebrity consumes every part of our life in some way. Now, I'm not saying that to assume that you're wanting to be a celebrity or some social media star. What I am saying though, is that deep down at some core level, we're all programmed to want likes. Simply, we all want to be liked. Likes go far beyond social media. Likes are much, much more than just the thumbs up on Facebook. If you're reading these words right now, at some core level, it's important to you that people like you. And it's alright, to be honest about that. We all do.

We live in such a celebrity driven culture that social media in some way influences every facet of our life, even when we're not fully conscious of it. We all want to be liked. Well, this desire to be liked takes on a life of its own when we think of the world of social media influencers. It's not just for the younger generation, it's for all of us, in fact. When was the last time you felt you just couldn't drift off to sleep without checking your news feed on Facebook? We've all been there. Maybe it's to check up on a friend or to see what that special someone is doing. In this fast-paced, celebrity driven culture, however, the desire to be liked takes on a life of its own.

I recently watched a documentary on the power of becoming a social media influencer. Today as never before people are becoming multimillionaires simply because they have the right profile in place. In fact, there are even companies that allow you to purchase likes, page views and responses and comments on your social media pages. Although there's nothing altogether wrong with that, and it's a very powerful tool in business and branding and in marketing, what happens is many times in life we bring that same desire to be liked into our own natural lives. As a result, we always want to put our best foot forward. We censor ourselves. And somewhere in the mix of it all, somewhere it gets lost in translation power of genuineness.

As I said earlier, sometimes the very hardest thing to do is to be yourself. Especially in a world that tells you how you should be and how you should act. In a world of social media influencers, well, the truth is we're all influencing someone. We always want to be liked. But for a moment, I want you to take this idea and bring it into three-dimensional reality. Although you may not be buying likes on Facebook or Twitter or Instagram. At some level, whether you've realized it or not. You've really purchased likes throughout your own life. Day after day, at some level, you've paid some price for people to like you.

Maybe it was the time you censored yourself when you were asked a question by a friend. Maybe it's the time you lied when you were meeting that new special someone. Maybe it's the time you fudged the truth when your coworker asked how the new presentations coming along. Or remember the time when your boss asked if you were going to be able to work on the weekend? Remember your response? Well, it was a way to get his approval. In all these moments, you were buying "likes," whether you realize it or not.

It's time to return to the power of genuineness. As I felt the inspiration to write this book, I wanted to include this chapter as a way to say one of the most powerful things you'll ever do in life is yourself. Well, I'll be the first to admit it's much easier said than done. Now more than ever before, we're looking for likes. Most often, though, these likes come at a price. Many times, these likes that we're looking for come at the cost of our own sense of genuineness. I sometimes say that we even that now we don't even really know how to be ourselves any longer. Well, if you're looking for better relationships, stronger relationships, and more important connections, you're going to have to learn to realize the power of vulnerability.

It's time to remove the mask you've been wearing for far too long. It's time to let the world see you. The real you, that is. It's frightening, I'll admit. In fact, most often nothing stirs fear quite like the feeling of vulnerability. At some core level, it goes against everything we want.

What if he disagrees with me? What if she doesn't like what I think? What if the boss chooses someone else over me? What if my spouse won't understand? Can you relate in some way?

You see, whether you've ever taken the time to realize it or not, with all those moments of hesitation, you're considering buying likes. And in some way, you're giving up part of yourself to appease others. Somewhere in the mix of it all, what's lost in translation is the importance of genuineness. My friend, chances are you've worn a mask for so long, you've forgotten who you truly are. I wanted to include this chapter within the book to remind you. It's time to become more open.

Does the world know the real you? It's a very important question if you truly think about it. I mean the real you. I'm not asking about the idea of you the world has. Instead, I'm asking about the real you. Who you truly are. What do you truly like?

In order to build genuine, lasting true connections and true relationships, you're going to have to become a lot more vulnerable than you've been. You're going to have to give the world the opportunity to get to know who you truly are. Well, as frightening as it is, it's necessary. That is, if you want relationships that stand the test of time.

So often throughout countless coaching sessions, what I find with most people asking for love and relationships is that. The idea of openness. Is sometimes lost in translation. We want others to be open with us. In fact, let's be honest, we expect that openness from others. Most often, however, when it comes to us being open with them, we become more than a little frightened. To put it a lot more bluntly, sometimes where openness and vulnerability are concerned, we become hypocrites. We expect others to share the truth with us and live in openness the entire time. We ourselves fight against our own genuineness. As humans, we love to control the narrative. Suffice it to say, we love public perception and the ability that we must always control it.

As frightening as it is, however, something truly magical and heavenly begins to happen the moment you take on a sense of genuineness and openness. When you remove the mask and allow the world and those around you to see who you truly are, you might be surprised to find that they like what they say. Most often, once finally removing the mask, to our great surprise and to our great wonder, we find ourselves shocked that many people out there in the world accept us. Just the way we are. Although it's a great big world filled with many interesting and unique characters, many different people and much,

much diversity, the beautiful reality of existence is that there are other people who want to be accepted just the way they are. In that you are no different than anyone else on planet Earth. Where relationships are concerned, the truth is we're looking for a greater sense of relatability with others.

What if I were to tell you that right now, there are people in the world who are ready, willing, and able to accept you just the way you are? Would you find such a claim shocking? At first glance, it may seem unbelievable. It only feels this way though, because chances are you've not found those connections yet. Once you learn to remove the mask and finally be your true, authentic and genuine self, however, you'll begin to make these connections much more easily.

From platonic friendships to business dealings with coworkers and partners and business relationships, vulnerability and openness matter greatly. However, it seems we find the greatest reward of openness and vulnerability in our connections that are exist on a deeper level. Particularly where love and romance are concerned. Throughout the pages of this book, we've journeyed through relationships in many, many forms. The entire time, though, I'm sure you've been wondering, what about love and relationships? What about romance? Well, with the topic of romance is concerned, I've saved the very best for last. If you want to find true and lasting love and powerful romance in your life, you're going to have to learn the power of vulnerability. You're going to have to remove the mask that you've been afraid to take off for far too long.

Often when coaching couples seeking advice on love and relationships, or even in marriage, the topic that seems to come up most is the topic of openness. He just can't seem to share his feelings with me. Whenever she shares her feelings with me, it causes a fight. Jeremy, I made this new connection, and I just don't know what he's thinking. I met someone at the coffee shop last week and I'm so attracted to this person, but I just don't know what they're thinking. Is she really into me? All these things can be settled with a greater focus on vulnerability and openness. In fact, all the questions are answered the moment we come to the place of vulnerability.

What I mean to say is you're going to find all the relationships you've been dreaming about the moment you take off the mask. The moment you become a little more open with what you're truly feeling. The moment you move beyond the fear and step into the place of genuine vulnerability. It's frightening. And sometimes, as horrific as it might seem, the moment you take off the mask, you're going to find that in the place of genuine openness and vulnerability, you become much more easily able to express yourself. You'll communicate better. You'll open up more. And you won't be afraid to share your truth.

As simple as it sounds at first glance, have you ever stopped to think about how much confusion we bring to ourselves and our relationships simply because we're afraid of being vulnerable and open with others? Vulnerability you see is key. It's key where communication is concerned. And it's key where our emotions are concerned. It's time to start being a lot more genuine with what you truly think and feel. No more hiding. It's time to remove the mask.

What if I were to tell you that right now, there's someone in the world who wants you to be yourself? This goes far beyond just mere acceptance. As I said earlier, the world is filled right now with many people who are ready, willing and able to accept you for who you are. That's a very powerful, very beautiful thing if you think about it. But are you ready for something even more miraculous? Not only are there other people ready, willing and able to accept who you are, but there are people who want you to be yourself. These people are ready, willing, and able to accept you.

For far too long, you've been conditioned and programmed to believe that you can't really be yourself. As a result, you put on a mask, and you distance yourself from others. Because of this, even though you've made many connections in life, most of those connections haven't truly felt satisfying. Most of those relationships, in fact, sometimes haven't even felt very good at all. The reason for this is because you haven't been real. Well, it's time to get real.

The moment you become more able to take off the mask and become your genuine self and really put your true self out into the world, you're going to be shocked and amazed to find that there are people who will naturally gravitate towards you. They'll have the same interest, the same likes, many of the same passions. Like you, they'll be looking for something real themselves. Truly, in life, we're all connected in this way.

Right now, the world is filled with many, many interesting and remarkable people. We live in a world filled with such great and unique diversity. But in a world of such difference, and in a world in which everyone seems to be so very different from us. Where does that leave us where true relationships are concerned? Well, it leaves us in need of more vulnerability. The moment you become more open to the world, remove the mask and show the world your true self. You're going to be pleasantly surprised to say that there are others who love you just the way you are. If you truly want better and stronger relationships in life, start by being more open.

Chapter Nine

Giving Back

In the pages of this book, you and I have journeyed together into the deepest meanings of true, lasting relationships. We've covered relationships of all sorts. From platonic connections to familial connections, to partnerships in business and career. Even those of love and romance. And through it all, what I hope you've come away with Is that at the end of the day, the relationships we make in life will in some way mirror who we are. This is the power of the law of attraction at work. What we measure out to others, we will ultimately receive within our own lives.

But it's much more than just some divine universal principle. It's common sense if you truly think about it. What we do to others, we will have done to us. And not only is this a divine spiritual law, but it's also practicality in daily life. If you truly think about it when you ponder all the relationship connections you've made in life, chances are you're going to see this theme over and over again. That is, if you can learn to see the role that you've played in those connections.

Remember at the very beginning of this book when I shared there will be times when there will be difficult pills to swallow. That understanding the power of relationships will end some way cause us to hold a mirror to ourselves and confront some of the things about our own lives that we don't truly like. Well, the reason for this, quite simply, is because we're going to always receive what we give to others. If we don't have friends, it's because many times we haven't been very friendly ourselves. If we haven't received loyalty changes are it's because at some level, we haven't been loyal ourselves. If we find ourselves surrounded by people that we can't trust, will it says something about our own level of trustworthiness? It simply can't be stated enough that what we give to others, we will receive.

We find this theme all throughout the Scriptures also. I'm sure you've heard it said that we will always report we sell. Well, never is this any truer than where our relationships and life are concerned. Right now, in closing this book, I want to remind you of something very important. Your beliefs have always played a very central driving role in the formation of every connection you've ever made in life. In fact, if you truly take the time to think of it, you will admit that all of the connections you've made have in some way been a very important part of your own life, based on your own beliefs about yourself and other people. To put it another way, your relationships will always be determined by the way you view yourself and the way you view other people. Suffice it to say, our beliefs about relationships are very, very important.

But this goes far beyond just some mere metaphysical principle with an existence. In fact, it's part of life in every facet, each day. Whether it's passing a stranger on the street and offering a smile or holding the door open for someone behind you. The moments of action that we take in life will always have a direct correlation to the reactions we receive from other people. It's very practical if you truly think about it. Sometimes it's just simple as offering a tip to the delivery person. Which by the way, I hope you do.

Sometimes it's as simple as just offering a smile to the barista. She hands you your coffee during your morning commute to work. What I meant to say is that each day in life on planet Earth, we're always having these moments of encounter. We have so many moments of encounter, in fact, that usually we just casually dismiss them. Let's be honest, usually we're so very busy each day that we very rarely take the time to think about the importance of every random encounter. And let's be honest, they do most often seem very, very random, do they not? At first glance, it seems we're surrounded by strangers. People that we don't really know.

But maybe it's time to think of relationships in a much different way. From a much higher, more different perspective. What if I were to tell you that every person on planet Earth is a possible connection for you? That right now, even as you read these words, the world is filled with billions of people who in some ways are connected to you just because they exist. This is the power of oneness at work. I know on the surface of things it may seem that we're all so very, very different.

However, the truth is we have much more in common than we realize. When you learn to realize the power of Oneness and the importance of unity, not only will you begin to see relationships in a much different way, but you will begin to realize that people matter and that they serve a purpose in all our encounters.

As simple as it may seem at first glance, allow me to share it in a more relatable way. That random smile that you offered to the stranger, it meant a lot more to the stranger than you may realize. When you held the door open for the person behind you, it meant a lot more to the person behind you than you may consider. When you showed a spirit of true, genuine generosity in. In giving to the server at the restaurant, I promise you it made an impact. In the moment, it may have seemed as though she was just a server bringing you your food. However, maybe she was a single mother, raising three children and having to find a babysitter to even come to work. I promise you your spirit of generosity made an impact.

You see, it's time to think of relationships in a much more spiritual way than we typically do. Well, that is if we're going to truly begin to value relationships within our lives. This is where the real power of attraction comes into play. When we begin to honor people, we will begin to be connected to people of substance. In other words, to have relationships, true and lasting substance, we ourselves must begin living lives of quality and substance. But surprisingly, it goes even beyond this.

Can I now share with you perhaps the most shocking truth of all as it comes to relationships? What if I were to tell you that there really are no strangers at all on planet Earth? What if every single person in existence, in life, on planet Earth is connected to you already? What if we really have a connection that transcends any of our differences? What would this mean where our relationships are truly concerned?

There's a reason you interact as well as you do with certain people. There's a reason you feel a sense of commonality with certain individuals. It's not simply because you like certain people. No, no, it's much more than that. It's not even simply because you're friendly at times. It's because life will always attract like. All throughout life is the scripture to remind us of the deep is calling unto the deep. To put it another way, quite simply, energy always recognizes energy. And everything in existence, after all, really is just that. It's just energy.

So, all you're on your way to your evening workout and you happen to see the stranger on the subway, the one who catches your eye? Well, it's not just a moment of attraction, it's an exchange of energy. Or when you're sitting in the coffee shop with a friend and you look over and happen to see someone whose eyes are just glaring at you, someone who's just can't seem to take their eyes away from you. It's not just a moment of attraction, it's literal energy. There's a reason you notice the people that you notice. And by the same principle, there's a reason why certain people have always noticed you. It's more than just physical attraction, although you are very beautiful, I'm sure. It's energy.

Some call it intuition. Some call it vibes. Some even refer to it as that sixth sense that you keep hearing about. However, regardless of the terminology you choose to use, and no matter what you call it, we're always connecting with others around us on an energetic level. It's as if the soul seems to know in some way who we need within our lives and within our circles. It's this way by divine design. In the very beginning, when the creator formed in fashion, man from the dust of the Earth gave to him a help mate and said that it's not good for man to be alone. Well, in the very beginning of things, the Creator had relationships on his mind. That principle of relationship is still in effect. It never ended. It never stopped.

I share this to inspire you to begin to view your relationships in a much more spiritual, more energetic way. What may seem like trouble with coworkers or with the boss, it's not just a moment of tension, it's an energy exchange. The same could be said of moments of tension with a spouse or a partner. In all our dealings with people and life on planet Earth, everything is energy. So, knowing this, it's important to have a better understanding of what you're actually giving to the world around you. There's a reason you're making the attractive connections that you are. The reason simply is because you're putting out a very certain energy. The universe and the

Kingdom of heaven respond to the energy we put into existence. We do this through the thoughts we think.

There was a reason why Jesus, when sharing the message of the Kingdom of God to all those early believers, spoke so much of the power of belief. As I've said many times before, Jesus wholeheartedly believed in the power of the law of attraction. In fact, he even taught the law of attraction. He called it faith.

As Jesus went about doing good and healing all who were oppressed, he shared a very powerful principle concerning belief. He reminded all who would listen that at the end of the day, we're given exactly what we believe. Well, it really is a principle in existence if you truly think about it. Just as right now, all your life is the result of the beliefs you've held to, so too are the relationships in your life existing around you based entirely on your beliefs. Let's face it, as people, we form connections based on what we believe about people. And on the same token, we form relationship connections based on what we truly believe about ourselves. Weather from a feeling of worthiness or sense of unworthiness.

As you've read this book, what I hope you've realized and begun to take away from it, is the fact that all our relationship connections in life exist on purpose. There's no such thing as an accidental connection. And really, there's no such thing as strangers. We're all part of the beautiful human family designed and created by God. And all our differences aside, there's really much more in common than we realize. At the end of the day, when we think of the topic of relationships, what we're referring to as a sense of relatability. We're all looking for ways to relate. We want to relate to others into the world around us.

Where we so often miss it, though, is that we sometimes casually dismiss or disregard the role that we ourselves have been given to play in all these important connections we make. We seem to pass the buck where energy exchange is concerned. In this sense, we sort of become literal energy vampires. We always seem so concerned with what we're receiving from others, but rarely do we ever stop to think of the energy we're putting out into the world around us. Often, we view relationships from the perspective of taking rather than giving. This is why so many of the connections we make at times seem less than satisfying.

It's time to become more conscientious and more cognizant of the energy you're putting into the connections around you. In other words, it's time to become a little more thoughtful. To have true and lasting relationships, better, stronger relationships, you're going to have to realize that there's an energy at work. The energy stems from what you're believing about other people. And, it's time from what you're believing about yourself.

Personally, I happen to find that when viewing relationship connections from this more heavenly, more divine, more energetic perspective, suddenly the connections I make seem a lot more rewarding and a lot more fulfilling. You appreciate relationship connections much, much more once you realize that those connections haven't come by happenstance or by coincidence. After all, did the Scriptures not remind us that all things work together for our good? Well, if we truly believe that we must also see that relationships are made for our good. In other words, even when they may not feel good, there's always a greater meaning and purpose behind the connection. When you start to realize that no coincidence exists, you'll begin to view relationships in a much different way.

Not only does life become much more beautiful when you realize that relationships are divine. But you start to realize the beauty of people as well. It becomes a lot more difficult to judge someone once you realize they're looking for the same things in life than you are. It becomes much more difficult to just casually dismiss someone when you realize that they're looking for relatability as well. Well, if you think about it, that's the perfect way to close this book. When we talk about the power of relationships, what would truly meaning is that we're looking for a sense of relatability, relatability to each other and relatability to the world around us. So where building strong relationships is concerned, if you truly want better relationships, you're going to have to learn to relate to those connections in a different way than before. It really can't be stressed enough, but what we give to others is ultimately what we will receive. So, with that being said, here's to you having more connections that feel satisfying, and here's to you having a life of connections that truly have meaning.

Chapter Ten

"People Matter"

In a world that often emphasizes achievements, wealth, and status, it's crucial to remember that people matter. Every individual possesses inherent value and deserves to be treated with respect, empathy, and dignity. In this chapter, we will explore the importance of understanding and acknowledging the worth of each person you encounter. By embracing this mindset, you can cultivate meaningful relationships, foster a sense of compassion, and contribute to a more inclusive and harmonious society. People matter.

At the core of understanding the value of people lies the recognition that every individual is unique, possessing their own thoughts, emotions, and life experiences. Each person has their own dreams, aspirations, and struggles. It's essential to view others not merely as means to an end but as individuals with their own stories and inherent worth. By appreciating this, you open yourself up to a world of understanding and empathy.

To truly comprehend the value of people, it's vital to cultivate compassion and empathy. By putting yourself in someone else's shoes, you gain insight into their perspectives, challenges, and emotions. This understanding allows you to connect with others on a deeper level and provide support when they need it most. Compassion and empathy create a positive ripple effect, as your kindness and understanding can inspire others to do the same.

Recognizing the value of people fosters the development of authentic connections and meaningful relationships. When you genuinely acknowledge and appreciate others, you create an atmosphere of trust and mutual respect. These connections enrich your life, provide a support network, and enable personal and professional growth. Engaging in open and respectful conversations, actively listening, and seeking to understand others' viewpoints are essential components of building such connections.

Understanding that people matter involves embracing diversity and inclusion. Every individual brings a unique set of perspectives, skills, and talents to the table. By valuing diversity and creating an inclusive environment, you enable the flourishing of creativity, innovation, and collaboration. Embracing diversity also means recognizing and challenging biases, preconceptions, and stereotypes that may hinder our ability to see the inherent value in others.

When you recognize and appreciate the value of people, you inspire them to recognize their own worth as well. Your words and actions can lift others up, boost their self-esteem, and encourage them to pursue their passions. By affirming their value, you contribute to a positive and supportive community where everyone can thrive. Remember, small acts of kindness and validation can have a profound impact on someone's life.

Understanding that people matter and have value is a foundational principle for building a compassionate and inclusive world. By recognizing the uniqueness and worth of each individual, practicing empathy and compassion, and embracing diversity, you create an environment that fosters personal growth, meaningful connections, and positive change. As you embark on this journey, always remember that the way you treat others has the power to shape their lives and leave a lasting impact.

One of the challenges in recognizing the value of people is overcoming judgment and preconceived notions. We often make assumptions based on appearances, social status, or other superficial factors. However, true understanding requires looking beyond these initial impressions and taking the time to know someone on a deeper level. By challenging your own biases and giving others a fair chance, you open yourself up to discovering the hidden potential and worth in every person.

To fully appreciate the value of people, it's important to adopt a growth mindset. This mindset emphasizes the belief that individuals have the capacity to learn, grow, and change. When you see others as capable of development, you become more patient and understanding. Instead of dismissing someone's shortcomings, you see them as opportunities for growth and support. Encouraging and empowering others to reach their full potential not only benefits them but also enriches your own life.

Listening actively is a powerful way to demonstrate that you value someone's thoughts, feelings, and experiences. When engaging in conversation, practice active listening by giving your full attention, maintaining eye contact, and refraining from interrupting. Validate their emotions and experiences by acknowledging their feelings and providing support. By being present and attentive, you show that their words and perspectives matter.

Understanding that people matter means recognizing the impact of small acts of kindness. Simple gestures like a smile, a kind word, or a helping hand can make a significant difference in someone's day. Never underestimate the power of your actions, as they have the potential to brighten someone's life, restore their faith in humanity, and remind them of their own value.

To promote the understanding that people matter, it's essential to lead by example. Be conscious of your own words and actions, ensuring that they align with the values of empathy, respect, and inclusivity. Show others how to value people by treating everyone you encounter with kindness and dignity. When others witness your behavior, they are more likely to emulate it, creating a positive cycle of compassion and understanding.

Understanding and acknowledging the value of people is a transformative mindset that can bring about profound change in both personal relationships and the world at large. By recognizing the uniqueness, worth, and potential of every individual, we create a society that values compassion, empathy, and inclusivity. As you navigate through life, remember that by valuing others, you not only enrich their lives but also contribute to your own growth and fulfillment. Embrace this understanding and become a catalyst for positive change, one person at a time.

Understanding that people matter involves celebrating the diverse strengths and talents that each individual possesses. Instead of viewing differences as barriers, embrace them as opportunities for growth and learning. Recognize that every person brings something unique to the table, whether it's their skills, experiences, or perspectives. By fostering an environment that values and celebrates these differences, you create space for collaboration, innovation, and collective progress.

While it's crucial to recognize the worth of others, it's equally important to extend that empathy and understanding to ourselves. Often, we can be our harshest critics, downplaying our own value and worth. By practicing self-compassion, we acknowledge our own needs, emotions, and aspirations. This self-acceptance allows us to approach others with a genuine sense of empathy and kindness, creating stronger connections based on mutual understanding and respect.

Understanding the value of people goes beyond individual interactions. It extends to cultivating a sense of community and collective responsibility. Recognize that we are all interconnected and that our actions have ripple effects on those around us. By actively participating in community initiatives, supporting social causes, and fostering inclusivity, we contribute to building a society that values and uplifts every member.

Each person we encounter holds a wealth of knowledge and experiences that we can learn from. Embracing the value of people means being open to different perspectives, cultures, and ideas. Engage in meaningful conversations, ask questions, and be curious about the lives and journeys of others. By seeking to understand, we broaden our own horizons, challenge our preconceptions, and foster personal growth.

In our increasingly digital world, it's important to remember the power of genuine human connection. While technology can facilitate communication, it's the depth of personal interactions that truly makes a difference. Take the time to engage in face-to-face conversations, build relationships, and create moments of genuine connection. By actively investing in these interactions, we affirm the value and importance of people in our lives.

Understanding that people matter and have intrinsic value is a mindset that requires ongoing commitment and practice. By embracing empathy, compassion, and inclusivity, we create a world where every individual feels seen, heard, and valued. As you navigate your journey, keep in mind that the small acts of kindness, the genuine connections, and the efforts to understand others can have a profound impact on the lives of those around you. Together, let us champion the worth of people and contribute to a more compassionate and harmonious world.

In a world filled with billions of people, it's essential to recognize and celebrate the uniqueness that each individual brings. We are all different, shaped by our backgrounds, experiences, and perspectives. In this chapter, we will explore the beauty of diversity and how every person has something valuable to offer to the world. By embracing these differences and honoring individual contributions, we can create a more inclusive and enriching society.

Diversity is the fabric of our human existence. Each person is a mosaic of distinct qualities, including their cultural heritage, beliefs, skills, and talents. Our differences should be embraced, not feared or overlooked. They bring richness and depth to our collective human experience. By appreciating diversity, we open ourselves up to a world of new ideas, perspectives, and ways of living.

No two individuals see the world in the same way. Our diverse backgrounds and experiences shape our unique perspectives. When we engage with people who have different viewpoints, we gain a broader understanding of the world. Embracing these perspectives fosters creativity, innovation, and problem-solving. It allows us to approach challenges from multiple angles and find more comprehensive solutions.

Recognizing that everyone is different cultivates empathy and understanding. When we appreciate the variety of experiences and challenges others face, we develop a deeper sense of compassion. It becomes easier to connect with people on a human level and treat them with respect and kindness. Empathy enables us to bridge divides, dissolve stereotypes, and build bridges of understanding.

Each person possesses unique talents and abilities that are waiting to be discovered and shared with the world. By recognizing and encouraging these hidden talents, we unlock new potentials and enrich society. It is through embracing diversity that we create an environment that nurtures individual growth and allows these talents to flourish. Everyone has something valuable to contribute, whether it's through art, science, music, entrepreneurship, caregiving, or any other field.

When individuals with diverse backgrounds and skills come together, magic happens. Collaboration between people from different walks of life brings together a wealth of knowledge, experiences, and perspectives. It fosters synergy, where the collective efforts and strengths of individuals combine to create something greater than the sum of its parts. By recognizing and valuing the contributions of others, we unlock the full potential of collaboration.

In a diverse world, learning opportunities abound. Each interaction with someone different from us presents an opportunity to expand our knowledge and challenge our preconceptions. By embracing these learning opportunities, we grow as individuals and develop a broader understanding of the world. Embracing diversity means embracing a lifetime of learning, curiosity, and personal growth.

Recognizing and valuing the unique contributions of individuals allows us to create a society where everyone can thrive. By creating inclusive environments that celebrate diversity, we empower individuals to bring their best selves forward. This, in turn, leads to personal fulfillment, increased productivity, and positive societal change. The impact of embracing diversity extends beyond the individual—it ripples through communities, organizations, and the world at large.

In a world where we are all different, we all have something valuable to offer. Embracing diversity means recognizing and celebrating the uniqueness of each person. It means honoring their perspectives, talents, and contributions. By doing so, we create a society that is richer, more vibrant, and more inclusive. Let us cherish the diversity that surrounds us, learn from one another, and together, shape a world where every individual's value is appreciated and where we can all thrive.

Chapter Eleven

Divine Connections

Not only do people matter, but our connections to the people around us are divine connections. In our journey through life, we encounter countless individuals who leave lasting impressions on our hearts and minds. Some connections may be brief, while others are long-lasting and profound. But have you ever considered that every person you meet, every connection you forge, is a part of a grand design? In this chapter, we will explore the idea that all our connections to people are divine connections, orchestrated by a higher power that weaves together the tapestry of our lives.

Each person we meet is like a thread interwoven into the fabric of our existence. These threads cross our paths for a reason, bringing with them opportunities for growth, love, and learning. Sometimes, we encounter individuals who challenge us, pushing us to examine our beliefs and values. Other times, we meet kindred spirits who share our passions and dreams, igniting a spark within us. Whether positive or negative, every connection has a purpose in shaping our journey.

Every interaction we have with another person offers us a chance to practice empathy and compassion. When we truly listen to someone's story, we open our hearts to their joys, sorrows, and struggles. Through our connections, we learn to understand the diverse experiences and perspectives that make us uniquely human. In this way, our connections transcend the surface level and delve deep into the essence of our shared humanity.

Our connections to others often serve as mirrors, reflecting back to us aspects of ourselves that we may not have recognized otherwise. Sometimes, we find inspiration and guidance through the qualities we admire in others. At other times, we may encounter individuals who mirror our own flaws and challenges, urging us to confront and overcome them. These connections provide fertile ground for personal growth and self-discovery.

Perhaps the most profound aspect of our divine connections is the love that flows through them. Love has the power to heal, inspire, and transform our lives. When we connect with others on a soul level, we tap into the divine spark within ourselves and them. We recognize that we are all interconnected, and our love radiates outward, embracing the world around us. These connections remind us that we are never alone, and that love is the language of the divine.

Recognizing the divinity in our connections allows us to approach relationships with reverence, gratitude, and openness. It encourages us to be mindful of the impact we have on others and to cherish the gifts they bring into our lives. It also reminds us to trust in the synchronicity of the universe, understanding that each connection is a stepping stone on our unique path.

As we navigate the intricacies of human connections, let us remember that they are not mere coincidences but divinely orchestrated encounters. Each person we meet, whether fleeting or enduring, contributes to the tapestry of our lives in ways that are both profound and purposeful. So, embrace your connections, nurture them with love, and trust that the divine hand guides you on your journey, weaving together the threads of your destiny.

Sometimes, it may be challenging to see the divine nature of certain connections, especially during times of hardship or conflict. However, even in the most difficult encounters, there is wisdom to be gained. These connections may be catalysts for personal transformation, teaching us resilience, forgiveness, and the power of letting go. They push us to expand our understanding and embrace the inherent lessons that lie within every interaction.

Within the realm of divine connections, there exist sacred contracts and shared missions. Certain individuals are destined to cross our paths, serving as catalysts for our growth or as partners in fulfilling a common purpose. These connections may manifest as deep friendships, romantic relationships, or collaborations in various areas of life. Through shared experiences and joint efforts, we amplify our impact on the world and align with our higher callings.

Beyond the physical realm, there exists a spiritual dimension where our souls are intricately connected. We encounter members of our soul family, souls with whom we have shared past lives or a deep spiritual bond. These connections are often felt instantaneously, as if we have known each other for eternity. Soulmates, too, fall into this category—individuals who awaken our spirits, ignite our passions, and bring profound love into our lives. These connections remind us of the eternal nature of our souls and the interconnectedness of all beings.

Our connections to others can also serve as conduits for divine guidance and support. Sometimes, a chance encounter or a conversation with a stranger can offer the exact insight or guidance we need at a particular moment. It's as if the universe speaks through these individuals, delivering messages of hope, encouragement, or clarity. By remaining open and attuned to the divine, we can receive these blessings and recognize the divine presence in every connection.

In the realm of divine connections, time and space hold little significance. We may meet someone briefly, yet the impact they have on us can last a lifetime. Alternatively, we may encounter individuals with whom we feel an immediate connection, regardless of geographical or cultural barriers. These connections remind us that our souls are eternal and that the bonds we form can transcend the limitations of this physical existence.

As we navigate the sacred dance of connection, it is vital to honor the divine within ourselves and others. We can cultivate mindfulness, compassion, and gratitude as we interact with those who cross our paths. Each encounter becomes an opportunity to appreciate the unique gifts, perspectives, and wisdom that others bring into our lives. By doing so, we contribute to the collective elevation of consciousness and the realization of our shared divinity.

In the grand tapestry of life, every connection we forge is imbued with the divine. Each encounter carries the potential for growth, healing, and love. By recognizing the sacred nature of our connections, we open ourselves to the wisdom they hold, the lessons they offer, and the transformative power they possess. As we honor and embrace these connections, we embrace the interconnectedness of all beings and embark on a journey of self-discovery, spiritual evolution, and profound love.

The divine orchestration of our connections extends beyond the individuals themselves—it also encompasses the timing of these encounters. Often, we may question why certain connections happen when they do, especially if they seem to come at inconvenient or challenging moments. However, the divine hand at work knows precisely when to bring people into our lives. It may be to offer support during a difficult period, to provide guidance when we're at a crossroads, or to inspire us to step into our true purpose. Trusting in the timing of these connections allows us to surrender to the unfolding of our journeys and witness the magic that emerges.

The impact of our divine connections goes far beyond the immediate individuals involved. Just as a single drop creates ripples that spread across a vast body of water, our connections have the power to create a ripple effect of transformation. The insights, love, and growth that we experience in these connections can inspire us to become catalysts for positive change in the lives of others. As we embrace our divine connections, we contribute to the collective awakening and evolution of humanity.

Like any tapestry, our connections are subject to the ebb and flow of life. Some connections may endure for a lifetime, while others may fade away or evolve into different forms. It's essential to embrace the natural rhythms of these connections, allowing them to unfold organically. We must hold them with love and gratitude, whether they are meant to be temporary or everlasting. Trusting in the divine wisdom that governs our connections allows us to release any attachments and surrender to the divine plan.

Within the web of divine connections, there are sacred contracts that we enter into before our earthly journey. These contracts are agreements made at a soul level, outlining the lessons, growth, and experiences we are meant to encounter with specific individuals. Honoring these contracts means acknowledging the profound purpose and significance of each connection. It involves embracing the challenges, celebrating the joys, and offering gratitude for the opportunity to learn and evolve together.

Ultimately, as we recognize the divine nature of all our connections, we deepen our connection to the divine within ourselves. We come to understand that we are spiritual beings having a human experience, and our interactions with others are gateways to spiritual growth and realization. Each connection becomes an invitation to embody love, compassion, and understanding, allowing us to mirror the divine qualities that reside within us. In this way, our connections become a sacred path to self-realization and a deepening connection to the divine.

In the grand tapestry of life, our connections to people are threads that interweave our souls, guiding us toward growth, love, and self-discovery. Embracing the divine nature of these connections empowers us to navigate the dance of relationships with reverence, gratitude, and trust. As we honor the divine tapestry of human connections, we step into the flow of the universe, embracing the profound purpose and beauty that each connection brings. Remember, dear reader, that every encounter is an opportunity for divine grace to manifest, and within the tapestry of connections lies the infinite potential for spiritual evolution and the realization of our interconnected oneness.

As we delve deeper into the understanding of divine connections, we begin to recognize the power of co-creation and collaboration. Each person we encounter holds unique gifts, talents, and perspectives that contribute to the collective tapestry of humanity. Through collaboration, we can combine our strengths, knowledge, and resources to manifest a shared vision or bring forth positive change in the world. These connections remind us that we are not meant to walk this journey alone, but rather to join hands and hearts with others in a collective dance of creation.

Our divine connections serve as catalysts for expanding our consciousness and facilitating our spiritual growth. Through the interactions and relationships we forge, we are presented with opportunities to explore different aspects of ourselves, confront our fears and limitations, and embrace new levels of awareness. These connections become mirrors that reflect our inner landscape, guiding us toward self-discovery and a deeper understanding of our true essence. As we engage in soulful connections, we unlock the door to our own evolution and transformation.

Within the realm of divine connections, guidance and wisdom flow freely. The Universe speaks to us through the words, actions, and experiences of the people we encounter. It is in the stillness of our hearts and the openness of our minds that we can tune in to this guidance. Paying attention to synchronicities, intuitive nudges, and the lessons presented by those we connect with, we can navigate our paths with a greater sense of purpose and clarity. Trusting in the divine guidance that arises within our connections allows us to walk our unique journeys with grace and alignment.

The power of divine connections extends to our own healing and the healing of others. When we engage in authentic, heart-centered connections, we create spaces of acceptance, compassion, and love. Within these spaces, wounds are acknowledged, vulnerability is embraced, and profound healing can occur. Through the support and understanding offered by those we connect with, we can reclaim our wholeness, release past traumas, and step into the fullness of our being. In turn, we become instruments of healing for others, offering solace and transformation through our own divine connections.

Even as connections change and evolve, the essence of their divine nature remains constant. Some connections may shift from intense to gentle, from close to distant, but the impact they have had on our lives remains. The lessons, love, and growth that we have experienced through these connections become a part of our story and contribute to the tapestry of our existence. We carry the imprints of these connections within us, forever enriched by the divine touch they brought into our lives.

In the vast tapestry of human connections, we come to recognize that every encounter is divinely orchestrated. Whether brief or enduring, challenging or joyous, each connection serves a purpose in our spiritual evolution and the collective awakening of humanity. As we embrace the co-creative power, expand our consciousness, and honor the healing potential of our connections, we step into the flow of divine guidance and love. Remember, dear reader, you are an integral thread in this grand tapestry, and every connection you make is a sacred opportunity for growth, collaboration, and the realization of your highest potential. Embrace the divine nature of your connections, and allow them to weave a beautiful and meaningful story throughout your journey.

Conclusion

Several years ago, I had the idea to write a book that at the time didn't seem like a very big deal. Little did I realize at the time that it would go on to become one of my bestselling books. It was the summer of 2018, when I first began to consider the idea of writing a book on the topic of relationships. The reason, quite simply, was because for more than 20 years even then. The topic of relationships was something I found myself being asked almost daily. Through countless prophetic coaching calls and through training sessions and even through success coaching, it seemed the one thing that always came up most was the topic of relationships.

The book was titled *Attracting Your Godly Spouse*. Well, it was met with rave reviews. So much so that it also included a workbook and a complete package, offering insight into how to attract quality relationships. To this day, it's still one of my bestselling books. And even now, all this time later, the offices of Identity Network received daily testimonies of how the book changed their lives and caused people to start to view relationships in a different way.

However, I felt there was more to say. Because if you think about it, life is filled with many, many different types of relationships. Sure, there's love and romance. However, there are also platonic connections with friends, their family connections made. There are interactions and dealings with our coworkers and our bosses and those in our career paths. Suffice it to say, life is filled with many, many different types of unique and interesting connections. It isn't always just love and romance. Although that seems to be the most popular, I'll admit.

That's, in a sense, how this book, building strong relationships, came into existence. I wanted to take a deeper look at all the connections we make in life. In fact, I want to do in some way inspire you, the reader, to begin to realize that relationships exist on purpose. They don't happen by accident. They don't come coincidentally. All our connections in life come from divine design. My hope and prayer now is that as you've read the pages of this book, you realize that there truly are no coincidences. Every single connection in every relationship made is a moment of impact energetically.

The truth is, we live in a world filled with so much diversity. While you're writing the story of your life, your story is going to include many interesting and many unique characters. Characters from all walks of life. Well, these certain people, these characters, if you will exist within your story for a reason, and the overall outcome of your story will depend entirely on how you choose to relate to the people around you. So, where the topic of stronger relationship is concerned, the reality is if you want stronger relationships and relationships of better quality, you're going to have to begin to realize how you individually relate to those connections.

All too often our relationships seem a little one sided. Well, what I mean by that is that most often when we think of relationships, we think of what we're receiving from other people or of what they're giving to us. Rarely, if ever, do we ever stop to take the time to think of what we ourselves are contributing to the people around us. In other words, we sometimes forget the role that we ourselves have been given to play in forming new, meaningful connections. As a result, sometimes we become a little hypocritical.

We expect a lot from the people around us, but rarely do we ever take the time to stop and think of what we are contributing to those people.

Well, what I hope you've learned to take away from this book as of now, is that at the end of the day, our relationships will always in some way serve as a mirror to remind us of our own selves. This is the principle of the Kingdom and work, and it really is the power of the law of attraction if you think of it. Every moment of connection, every moment of attraction exists to teach us something about ourselves. That is, if there's a greater purpose to it all. And do we not claim to believe that? Do we not claim to believe that all things are working together for our good? Personally, I do believe that. And if this is the case, then what that truly means is that there are no accidental connections.

So right now, even as you read these words, chances are you may look to your life and the people in your life. And chances are those connections may feel a little less than satisfying. Maybe you want more romance. Maybe you want a greater confidant. Maybe you want someone else you can trust a little more. Well, I want you to see, though, that it's time to start looking at the people in your life in a different way. Less one sided, that means. It's time to start viewing the role that you yourself are playing in all the formations you make.

Personally, what I find within my own life is there's a great deal to be said about the power of personal responsibility. Honestly, it's human nature to want to skirt the issue. But at the end of the day, it really is true. What we give to others we will receive within our own lives. You can call it anything you'd like, cause and effect or reaping what we sow, but at the end of the day it's practicality, even in life on planet Earth. If you want friends, you're going to have to be more friendly. And if you want stronger relationships in your life, you're going to have to become more conscientious and much more cognizant of how you are choosing to relate to the world around you. Remember, there are no accidents and there are no coincidences.

And so, to put it another way, allow me to say that the people on planet Earth matter. They matter just as much as you do. Their unique experiences and the stories that they bring to life each day through every encounter serve a purpose. It's the same way that your story serves a purpose. What I found within my own life, and I continue to see myself reminded of time and time again, is that although we live in a world of such great diversity, there's much more in common than we realize. Just as you're looking for stronger relationships, so too is everyone else on planet Earth.

Everyone has something to offer. Everyone has a unique and beautiful divinely inspired story to share. And so, when you're thinking of the relationships in your life, remember that you two have been given a role to play. If you want stronger relationships in your life, lasting relationships, you're going to have to learn to relate to people more differently than you have. Truly, there really are no strangers. There are only endless possibilities. Possibilities for new connections, that is.

As we journey through life, we often encounter countless faces, unfamiliar and unknown. We label them as strangers, entities separate from ourselves. Yet, beneath the surface, there exists a profound truth: there are no strangers in this intricate tapestry we call life. We are all intricately connected, woven together by a web of shared experiences, emotions, and the universal essence of being human.

Every person we encounter, whether fleetingly or in deep connection, carries within them a unique story. Their thoughts, dreams, fears, and aspirations mirror our own. They, too, have walked paths strewn with joy and sorrow, faced triumphs and challenges, and sought meaning in a world that often defies our understanding. When we realize this fundamental truth, the concept of strangers begins to dissipate, replaced by a sense of kinship that transcends the boundaries of familiarity.

Consider the myriad of connections we share with others. In our daily lives, we interact with family, friends, colleagues, and neighbors, each representing a thread in the tapestry of our existence. But even beyond those closest to us, there lies an intricate network of connections waiting to be discovered. The person we sit beside on a crowded train, the stranger whose smile brightens our day, or the passerby whose life intersects with ours for a fleeting moment - each holds the potential for a profound exchange of humanity.

Through our shared experiences, we find common ground with those we may consider strangers. Think about the fundamental experiences we all undergo: the joy of laughter, the heartache of loss, the exhilaration of achievement, and the vulnerability of love. These emotions transcend language, culture, and geographical boundaries. When we open our hearts and minds to the universality of human experience, the barriers that separate us begin to crumble.

Moreover, the interconnectedness of our lives becomes even more apparent when we reflect upon the ripple effect of our actions. A single act of kindness can create a chain reaction, inspiring others to follow suit. By showing compassion to a stranger, we affirm our shared humanity and create a spark of connection that resonates far beyond that initial encounter. It is through these acts that we come to understand the far-reaching impact we have on the lives of others and the intricate network that binds us all.

To recognize the absence of strangers is to acknowledge the beauty of diversity. Each person we encounter brings a unique perspective, shaped by their experiences and beliefs. By embracing this diversity, we enrich our own understanding of the world. We discover new cultures, traditions, and ways of thinking that expand our horizons and challenge our preconceived notions. In this way, our connections with others become an opportunity for personal growth and enlightenment.

In the grand tapestry of life, every thread, no matter how seemingly insignificant, is essential. Each encounter, every connection, weaves together the fabric of our shared human experience. By nurturing empathy, compassion, and understanding, we deepen these connections and foster a world that transcends divisions and embraces the inherent oneness of humanity.

So, let us cast aside the notion of strangers and instead embrace the truth of our interconnectedness. Let us approach each encounter with curiosity, recognizing the potential for connection that lies within. As we walk this path of life, may we remember that we are all part of something much greater, a tapestry of connection that unites us all.

As we navigate the vast expanse of existence, it is essential to acknowledge that our interconnectedness extends beyond the realm of personal encounters. We are not only connected to those we meet in person but also to the countless lives and stories that have come before us and will follow in our wake.

Reflect for a moment on the shared history of humanity. From the ancient civilizations that shaped our world to the struggles and triumphs of our ancestors, their narratives are imprinted within us. We carry their genetic legacy, their cultural heritage, and the wisdom passed down through generations. In this sense, we are the embodiment of their dreams, hopes, and aspirations.

Consider the countless innovations and discoveries that have propelled our species forward. Every scientific breakthrough, every work of art, and every great idea is a product of collective inspiration. We stand on the shoulders of those who came before us, drawing inspiration from their contributions. The intellectual tapestry we contribute to is not an individual creation but a collaborative masterpiece that transcends time and space.

Furthermore, the natural world in which we exist is a testament to our interconnectedness. The delicate balance of ecosystems, the intricate web of life, and the symbiotic relationships that sustain our planet are all reminders of the interwoven nature of existence. The air we breathe, the water we drink, and the earth beneath our feet connect us to every living being, reminding us that our well-being is intertwined with the well-being of the entire planet.

In the digital age, our connections extend even further. Through the power of technology, we can bridge vast distances, connecting with individuals from all corners of the globe. The internet has become a vast network of shared knowledge and experiences, allowing us to connect, learn, and empathize with people we may never meet in person. Social media platforms, online communities, and virtual spaces provide us with avenues to exchange ideas, challenge our perspectives, and find common ground.

At times, it may be easy to lose sight of our interconnectedness. The distractions and demands of modern life can create a sense of isolation, making it easy to overlook the threads that bind us together. However, by cultivating awareness and intention, we can nurture our sense of connection.

We can start by approaching each encounter with openness and curiosity. By seeing the potential for connection in every interaction, we invite meaningful exchanges and the discovery of shared experiences. Simple acts of kindness, genuine smiles, and listening with empathy can create bridges of understanding that transcend differences.

Moreover, let us strive to recognize and appreciate the interconnectedness of all life. By cultivating a deep respect for nature and embracing sustainable practices, we contribute to the well-being of the planet and the intricate ecosystems that support us. By acknowledging our shared responsibility, we can work collectively to protect and preserve the natural world for future generations.

In the grand tapestry of life, there are no strangers—only connections waiting to be discovered. As we walk this journey, let us weave a story of compassion, understanding, and unity. By embracing the truth of our interconnectedness, we can transcend divisions, foster empathy, and create a world where the threads of connection bind us all in a shared tapestry of love and belonging.

As we delve deeper into the understanding of our interconnectedness, we begin to recognize that the threads of connection are not limited to the human realm alone. Our existence is intricately entwined with all living beings and the vast cosmos that surrounds us. From the smallest microorganism to the vastness of the universe, we are part of an awe-inspiring tapestry of life.

In the natural world, we find a profound reflection of our interconnectedness. The delicate balance of ecosystems demonstrates how each organism, no matter how seemingly insignificant, plays a crucial role in sustaining the web of life. The fluttering of a butterfly's wings can have far-reaching effects, just as our individual actions reverberate throughout the interconnected system of existence. Recognizing this interdependence awakens a sense of responsibility and stewardship towards our planet and all its inhabitants.

Moreover, the awe-inspiring cosmos invites us to contemplate our place in the grand scheme of things. We are stardust, born from the same cosmic processes that shaped galaxies, stars, and planets. The atoms within us have traveled through time and space, connecting us to the vastness of the universe. When we gaze at the night sky, we are reminded of the infinite possibilities and the interconnected nature of all creation.

On a spiritual level, various wisdom traditions have long embraced the notion of our interconnectedness. Indigenous cultures around the world have revered the Earth as a living entity, acknowledging our profound connection to the natural world. Eastern philosophies speak of the concept of "oneness," recognizing that the essence of who we are is interconnected with all that exists. Science, spirituality, and ancient wisdom converge in the understanding that we are not separate entities but integral parts of a unified whole.

In our daily lives, we can nurture this sense of connection by cultivating mindfulness and presence. By engaging fully in each moment and acknowledging the presence of others, we dissolve the illusion of separation. Through active listening and genuine curiosity, we open ourselves to the richness of diverse perspectives and the shared humanity that binds us. Small acts of kindness and compassion, extended to both humans and non-human beings, ripple through the tapestry of life, spreading warmth and unity.

Embracing our interconnectedness also entails embracing the inevitable impermanence of life. Just as the threads of a tapestry are woven together and eventually unravel, our individual journeys merge and diverge, creating an ever-evolving pattern. When we accept this impermanence, we can appreciate the ebb and flow of relationships, recognizing that even when physical connections change, the underlying bond of our shared existence remains.

As we traverse the intricacies of life, let us remember that there are no strangers in this grand tapestry of existence. We are all connected, from the depths of our being to the vastness of the cosmos. By nurturing our connections, celebrating our diversity, and embracing our shared humanity, we contribute to the vibrant fabric of life. In the tapestry of oneness, we find solace, inspiration, and the profound realization that we are never truly alone.

ABOUT THE AUTHOR

Dr. Jeremy Lopez is Founder and President of Identity Network and Now Is Your Moment. Identity Network is one of the world's leading prophetic resource sites, offering books, teachings, and courses to a global audience. For more than thirty years, Dr. Lopez has been considered a pioneering voice within the field of the prophetic arts and his proven strategies for success coaching are now being implemented by various training groups and faith groups throughout the world. Dr. Lopez is the author of more than forty books, including his international bestselling books The Universe is at Your Command and Creating with Your Thoughts. Throughout his career, he has spoken prophetically into the lives of heads of business as well as heads of state. He has ministered to Governor Bob Riley of the State of Alabama, Prime Minister Benjamin Netanyahu, and Shimon Peres. Dr. Lopez continues to be a highly sought conference teacher and host, speaking on the topics of human potential and spirituality.

ADDITIONAL WORKS

Prophetic Transformation

The Universe is at Your Command: Vibrating the Creative Side of God

Creating with Your Thoughts

Creating Your Soul Map: Manifesting the Future You with a Vision Board

Creating Your Soul Map: A Visionary Workbook

Abandoned to Divine Destiny

The Law of Attraction: Universal Power of Spirit

The Gospel of Manipulation

SEERS: The Eyes of the Kingdom

Made in the USA
Columbia, SC
27 July 2024